THE
LAW OF LIBERTY
IN THE SPIRITUAL LIFE

Jo
Natalie
Above all be
a lover of Christ
Christmas '99

Joseph Barrall

THE
LAW OF LIBERTY
IN THE SPIRITUAL LIFE

BY

EVAN H. HOPKINS

WITH AN APPRECIATION BY
FRED MITCHELL

CHRISTIAN • LITERATURE • CRUSADE
Fort Washington, Pennsylvania 19034

CHRISTIAN LITERATURE CRUSADE

U.S.A.
P.O. Box 1449, Fort Washington, PA 19034

GREAT BRITAIN
51 The Dean, Alresford, Hants. SO24 9BJ

First American Edition
Edited and reset
1991

ISBN 0-87508-273-4

CONTENTS

EVAN HOPKINS

A UNIQUE GIFT TO KESWICK
AND THE CHURCH

" A LIFE so rich in influence for God and holiness," is Bishop Handley Moule's natural and spontaneous description of Evan Henry Hopkins—and Bishop Moule was too restrained a man to write extravagant estimates. Such, then, was the man who wrote this classic book on the holy life, which, lacking anything more technical and elaborate, has been rightly regarded as the textbook of the Keswick Convention, which has been such a blessing to the whole Church of God since 1875.

Evan Henry Hopkins was born on September 16, 1837, in the town of Santa Ana, in New Granada (now Colombia), South America, where his parents were then living, for his father's duties as a civil engineer had taken him to survey and supervise the silver mine near that town.

The family returned from South America to England in 1848, the author of *The Law of Liberty in the Spiritual Life* and his sisters all speaking Spanish as well as English. For a few years young Evan Henry Hopkins attended a private school in Bristol, but when he reached the age of fourteen the family was once again on the move, this time to Australia, where his education was continued at the Melbourne Academy. At eighteen he entered the College of Chemistry in that city, and afterwards went on to the Government School of Mines, evidently marked out to follow his father in a scientific career. But God had other plans.

The early Christian impressions upon him did not appear to be deep. He was confirmed by Bishop Blomfield, and while carrying out a scientific survey in the Isle of Man lodged with a godly Methodist who spoke to him about the grace of God. But it was not until 1858 that, returning from the Isle of Man and settled in Dorsetshire, the light broke upon his soul. It was in this southern English county, while he was engaged in both the oversight of property and in geological research, that a simple coastguardsman became Evangelist and pointed young Hopkins to the Lord. This coastguardsman had himself been converted only the day before, but he began early as a fisher of men— and what a catch on the second day of his new life! Mr. Marshallsay, the coastguardsman, told Evan Hopkins how the Lord had saved him the previous day while he was at work. He impressed upon Hopkins the text: "The blood of Jesus Christ, His Son, cleanseth us from all sin," and the young scientist was born again. Then the older man invited his young friend to kneel on the beach, where he tried to pray and could not: but on his way home the assurance was given that he was accepted by God for Christ's sake.

Evan Henry Hopkins was a new man in Christ; and

soon the district began to know that fact. Life was full of interest and his prospects were bright, but he was very soon made aware that the hand of God was upon him, directing him to prepare for the ministry of the Church of England. He therefore went to study divinity at King's College, London, where he had the great privilege of sitting at the feet of that fine professor and scholar Edward Hayes Plumptre, who introduced him to the treasures of New Testament study. It was here that the foundations were laid of his knowledge of Scripture which was to serve him so well in coming days.

During his year of theological study Hopkins was drawn into the deep evangelistic work which, at that time, was telling on the life of London. In Silvertown, among the employees of the large factories, he found his field of service, and there, after his ordination, he continued as curate of St. Mark's Church, Victoria Docks.

In June, 1865, Evan Hopkins, then twenty-eight years of age, was ordained deacon in St. Paul's Cathedral, by Dr. Tait, Bishop of London, and in the following year received his priest's orders.

In February, 1868, he moved to West London, becoming curate at Portman Chapel—now St. Paul's, Portman-square—where he had a fine senior colleague and guide of true evangelical persuasion. Here he found himself in the company of such worshipers as Lord Cairns and Lord Shaftesbury, and he soon became a help to these illustrious men, as well as acceptable to them.

Evan Hopkins' great and lasting ministry in a church

began after his marriage to Isabella Sarah Kitchin, of Hampton-on-Thames, when he left London for Richmond and became the first vicar of Holy Trinity, a church long associated with his name. From 1870 to 1893 Richmond was his home and the center of his work. Here he preached the gospel and expounded the Scriptures, seeing God both save sinners and edify saints.

It was in Curzon Chapel, Mayfair, London, on May Day, 1873, that a crisis took place which ever in his mind ranked next to that of his conversion years before on a Dorset beach. Robert Pearsall Smith, an American Quaker, was in England giving Bible readings on the Christian life, and showing that sanctification as well as justification was by faith, and that there were promises made by God which needed to be realized which would completely change the Christian's life. Mrs. Evan Hopkins describes the result of the meeting as follows:

"How well I recall his coming home, deeply moved by what he had heard and experienced! He told me that he was like one looking out on a land wide and beautiful, flowing with milk and honey. It was to be posessed. It was his. As he described it all, I felt that he had received an overflowing blessing, far beyond anything that I knew; and it seemed as if a gulf had come between us. We sat up late that evening, talking, with our Bibles before us. Oh, I was so hungry. At last, quite simply, but very really, I too took God at His word and accepted Christ as my indwelling Lord and Life, and believed that He did enthrone Himself in my heart."

It is not surprising, therefore, that when the Broadlands Convention was convened the following year (1874) Evan Hopkins was present, giving clear and definite teaching on the life of holiness. His scientific training and his New Testament studies were already being welded together for the glory of God.

Of Broadlands, much might be written—and of the Oxford Conventions of 1874 and the Brighton Convention of 1875; but we need only note that Evan Hopkins was being led into the middle of a stream of blessing which in the summer of 1875 gave rise to the first of those fruitful Conventions at Keswick which continue to this day.

From those beginnings until his last Keswick Convention in 1915, Evan Hopkins was one of the leading teachers and exponents of the teaching of the Convention, namely, "holiness by faith in Jesus, not by effort of my own," to quote Frances Ridley Havergal. His clear grasp of the truth, his intimate knowledge of Scripture, his mastery of assembly, his ability to lead inquirers to count on the promises, his simple but effective handling of an after-meeting, all continued to make him God's unique gift to Keswick and to the Church of God.

Mr. Hopkins passed away in 1918.

Evan Hopkins' teaching is set before the thoughtful reader in this, his greatest book, *The Law of Liberty in the Spiritual Life*. Its present reissue is timely and full of encouragement. There is a deep longing for a more intimate and personal knowledge of the exceeding great grace of God, and this book will surely be used to lead souls into blessing.

I began this sketch with a brief quotation from his friend, saintly Bishop Moule, and I conclude it with another quotation, a kind of summary, from the same skillful pen. "I learned to know him on many sides: his varied wealth of information, his exquisite water-color art, his perfectly charming cheerfulness, his humor, his large wisdom, always sympathetic, always sane, always animated by singleness of aim towards his Master's glory and his fellow-believer's good. And I saw something of the fair light and sweetness of his Christian home. He is gone. Having beautifully and nobly served his generation in the will of God, he has fallen asleep. And my life, for one of thousands, seems the poorer for his translation. But unless all things are a delusion (and they are not), Evan Hopkins' doctrine and witness about Christ and His holiness are everlastingly true."

It is because his teaching is true that we commend it, as taught so clearly in this volume.

FRED MITCHELL
General Director, China Inland Mission
Chairman, Keswick Convention Council
1952

Sin is the transgression of the law (1 John 3:4).

All unrighteouness is sin (1 John 5:17).

Let not sin therefore reign in your mortal body, that ye should obey it in the lusts thereof (Romans 6:12).

Wash me throughly from mine iniquity, and cleanse me from my sin (Psalm 51:2).

Who gave Himself for us, that He might redeem us from all iniquity, and purify unto Himself a peculiar people, zealous of good works (Titus 2:14).

Heal my soul: for I have sinned against Thee (Psalm 41:4).

I will heal their backsliding (Hosea 14:4).

Forasmuch as ye know that ye were not redeemed with corruptible things, as silver and gold, from your vain conversation received by tradition from your fathers; but with the precious blood of Christ, as of a lamb without blemish and without spot (1 Peter 1:18–19).

Now unto Him that is able to keep you from falling, and to present you faultless before the presence of His glory with exceeding joy, to the only wise God our Saviour, be glory and majesty, dominion and power, both now and ever. Amen (Jude 24–25).

1

SIN

EVERY heresy, it has been said, has its root in defective views of sin. What we think of the Atonement depends greatly upon what we think of the evil which made that Atonement necessary. The converse, no doubt, is also true. But if we would rise towards a full appreciation of the value of that infinite sacrifice, we must seek to understand, as perfectly as possible, the true nature of sin.

What then is sin? So widespread and universal is the existence of evil that we are apt to regard it as an inseparable adjunct to our human nature. But sin is not an essential element in the constitution of our humanity. We know that it was not in man originally, nor will it be in man as finally glorified; neither did it exist in the Man Christ Jesus. And yet there is scarcely a fact of which we are more conscious than the presence of evil. It meets us on every hand. Its desolating influence is seen and felt by all. Sin is no mere figment of the imagination; it is a terrible reality. It is no vague, indefinite shadow; it is a real and specific evil.

Nor again are we to regard sin as a necessary constituent of our moral progress. That it is overruled for our good, and that it is made to serve in the process of our spiritual discipline, is undoubtedly true, but sin is not an essential element in our moral training or spiritual advancement. *We need not sin that grace may abound; we need not be under its power, nor defiled by its taint, in order to be advancing in knowledge or growing in humility.*

To learn sin's true nature we must look at it, not only in relation to ourselves, but in relation to God; we must regard it in connection with His infinite justice, and holiness and love. It is only in that light that we shall understand its real character.

We must consider it, moreover, in more than one aspect. It is such a vast evil that we can form no adequate conception of its nature unless we look at it from various points of view. Sin has many aspects.

But from whatever side we contemplate it, we shall see that the characteristic feature of each aspect is met by a corresponding fitness in the remedy which God has provided for sin.

It is one thing to recognize the effects of sin on mankind; it is another thing to see it in its essential character, as rebellion against God. Man through sin has not only become "wounded and debilitated," he has become alienated from God; he has been brought into an attitude of positive antagonism to God. Sin therefore is not something which appeals to pity only, a mere misfortune; it is that which deserves punishment, for it is rebellion against the purity and goodness and majesty of God.

If sin were not an offence, we could conceive of the

mercy of God forgiving sin without any sacrifice; but the necessity of a sacrifice teaches us that sin is a violation of God's law. This necessity is set forth with unmistakable clearness in the Old Testament, and with equal emphasis in the New.

"Sin is the transgression of the law" (1 John 3:4). By the law we are to understand, "not only the Mosaic law of the Old Testament, but also the law of the New Testament in Christ, and by Him explained in word and exhibited in life, as the law written in man's heart for his special direction; it embraces the whole complex commandment" (Pearson).

Man feels within himself just what God has revealed in His Word—that sin needs something more than the mercy of God. In this respect the doctrine of the Bible and the witness of the human heart are one.

It is a true instinct of man's nature that teaches him that guilt needs compensation; but the mistake into which he falls, if left to himself, is that he seeks to make that compensation by means which he himself has devised. This is the history of all heathen sacrifices.

Sin is an offence because it is rebellion against the sovereignty of God, a contradiction to His nature, an insult to His holiness. It stands related to law—not merely to the law of reason, or of conscience, or of expediency, but to the law of God. Sin consists essentially in the lack of conformity to the will of God, which the law reveals; it is lawlessness—a breach of law. And thus, it is the law that reveals the sinfulness of sin. "The crookedness of a crooked line may be seen of itself, but it is still more evident if compared with a perfect standard of straightness."

While the voice of conscience tells us that some amends is needed for the guilt of our sin, it is only revelation that shows us how that amends can be made; it is only there that we learn *what* sacrifice is sufficient to atone for human guilt. This view of sin leads us to see the meaning of Christ's death on the cross. It was the death of a condemned criminal: "He was wounded for our transgressions, He was bruised for our iniquities" (Isaiah 53:5); He died, "the just for the unjust" (1 Peter 3:18).

Freedom from sin as a transgression, as an offence against God, consists then in this—that through Christ's atoning death it is so "put away" as "to make it as though it had never been." "No power in earth or heaven can make that not to have been done which has been done; the only imaginable and conceivable alteration is that it should be as *though* it had never been done, that all bad effects of it should be destroyed and obliterated, and that the sin should be nullified by compensation" (Mozley). This freedom from sin as an offence we enter into as a present privilege. It is the first aspect of liberty which we are brought to experience through a saving view of Christ's death upon the cross.

Sometimes the term sin is used in Scripture as having reference to *acts* of sin. This, however, is not the only sense in which sin is spoken of. It is also referred to as a power, dwelling and working in man.

When we speak of *sinning* we imply, of course, an action. But by an action we do not mean merely that which is external; it may be a purely inward one. Transgression therefore must not be limited to outward violations of God's law; it includes all those inner activities of the soul which are opposed to the mind and character of God.

In the sixth of Romans the particular aspect in which sin is contemplated is that of a ruling power. Sin is there personified as one who seeks to have lordship over the believer.

Consider what it is that the Fall has involved. It has not only brought upon man the penalty due to sin as an offence, it has enslaved him under sin as a ruling principle. Sin is a power that has entered into the central citadel of a man's being, and, establishing itself there, has brought every part of his nature under its sway. Sin is a principle that is essentially opposed to God, and by taking possession of man's will and affections makes him an enemy to God and leads him out into open rebellion against Him. Man has thus become a slave to sin.

From the central part of our nature sin reigns over the whole man. Our *body* is thus "the body of sin" (Romans 6:6). That is, "the body of [belonging to] sin"—"The material body . . . as the inlet of temptation and the agent of sin" (Dean Vaughan): for while we are under sin's dominion, the body is the instrument through which sin carries out its work; it is in sin's possession and under sin's control.

In this sixth chapter of Romans the apostle sets forth the believer's present position in reference to sin. The crucifixion of Christ has completely changed his relation to sin. Christ's death, which has separated the believer from the consequences of sin as a transgression, has also separated him from the authority of sin as a master—set him free.

The believer sees that Christ by dying for him has completely delivered him from the penalty of sin. So it is his privilege to see that because he is identified with Christ in that death, he is also delivered from sin as a ruling principle. Its power is broken. He is in that sense "free from sin" (Romans 6:18, 22).

The purpose of the apostle, in this sixth chapter, is to show how completely the believer is identified with Christ when "He died unto sin." To enter fully into the meaning of that death is to see that Christ has emancipated us from any further dealings with our old master, sin. The believer is privileged thus to take his place in Christ, who is now "alive unto God." From that standpoint he is henceforth to regard sin. He is now and for ever free from the old service and the old rule. The Cross has terminated the connection once for all, and terminated it abruptly. It has effected a definite and complete rupture with the old master, sin.

"Such is the divine secret of Christian sanctification, which distinguishes it profoundly from simple natural morality. The latter says to man, Become what thou wouldest be. The former says to the believer, Become what thou *art* already (in Christ). It puts a positive fact at the foundation of moral effort, to which the believer can return and have recourse anew at every instant. And this is the reason why his labor is not lost in barren aspiration, and does not end in despair.

"The believer does not get disentangled from sin gradually; he breaks with it in Christ once for all. He is placed by a decisive act of will in the sphere of perfect holiness, and it is within it that the gradual renewing of the personal life goes forward. This second gospel para-

dox, sanctification by faith, rests on the first, justification by faith" (Professor Godet on Romans 6).

The Cross is the efficient cause of this deliverance. Freedom from sin's ruling power is the immediate privilege of every believer. It is the essential condition or starting point of true service, as well as of real progress. Such service and growth are as possible for the young convert as for the mature believer. Therefore freedom from sin's dominion is a blessing we may claim by faith, just as we accept pardon. We may claim it as that which Christ has purchased for us, obtained for our immediate acceptance. We may go forth as set free from sin, and as alive unto God in Jesus Christ our Lord. This is freedom from sin as a ruling principle.

Unfortunately, it is possible to see in the death of Christ an all-sufficient atonement for sin and yet not to see that in that death we have also the secret or source of personal purification from sin.

Sin is not merely a load that weighs us down, or an offence that has brought upon us penal consequences. It is an uncleanness that makes us unfit for God's presence. We may have rejoiced in the fact that the load is gone, that the guilt has been atoned for, and yet we may know but little of Christ's power to cleanse. Owing even to one single act of disobedience we may have been thrown out of communion with our Lord. We have thus become conscious, not only of guilt, but of defilement.

How vividly all this comes out in God's dealings with Israel under the old covenant!

It is impossible to read the Book of Leviticus, for example, without being struck with the emphasis there laid on the necessity of being separated from ceremonial defilement. We notice in the directions there given how jealously Jehovah watched over His people in this matter. The most minute details are entered into respecting their food, their raiment, their habits, and other domestic arrangements. All this we know was significant of something far deeper than that which was merely physical or ceremonial. It is in the light of the gospel that we learn their full and true import.

Looking at the whole question of defilement, we notice that it arose from two distinct sources—external and internal.

The defilement that arose from within is chiefly dwelt upon in the Book of Leviticus. This has reference to the moral defilement that springs from indwelling evil. And the defilement that arose from without, through external contact with death, is brought out more especially in the Book of Numbers. There we have in type the defiling effects incurred by contact with the world.

In reference to the former, defilement arising from within, the most striking picture is that presented by the leper. Nothing could more forcibly impress Israel of old with the loathsome nature of sin than this fearful disease.

Such a one would be excluded from the sanctuary. He was shut out from the worship of God, and from all dealings with the people of God.

So with the man who had come in contact with death (Numbers 19), whether intentionally, through negligence, or unconsciously. He became at once ceremonially unclean, and was "cut off" from all the privileges of a redeemed worshiper.

Is it not so now?

The body in these types stands as an image of the soul. Ceremonial defilement and cleansing represented the spiritual pollution and purification revealed to us in the gospel.

The suspension of a believer's communion is that which answers to the cutting off of a member from the congregation of Israel.

In all these pictorial unfoldings of the gospel, God was teaching His redeemed people that He could not tolerate any uncleanness upon those whom He had brought unto Himself, and among whom He had taken up His abode. And because He required His people to be holy He made a special provision for their purification.

Whether we speak of the defilement that comes from within or that which arises from without, God had provided means by which all uncleanness might be ceremonially removed. And this provision God made with this view, that His people might walk before Him in close and abiding fellowship.

Now if such privileges were real under the Old Testament dispensation, how much more real are they under the New!

We must never lose sight of this central fact, that the true basis of all purification is found in the atoning death of Christ. There are not two fountains, two sources of life and purity. There is but one central spring, and that is the Cross.

It was to this both rites pointed—the law relating to the cleansing of the leper, and the ordinance of the red heifer. The place where the forgiveness of sins is found is also the source whence cleansing from defilement is obtained.

It was by a definite and personal appropriation of the divinely appointed provision that both the leper and the man who had come in contact with death were cleansed and restored to fellowship with God. Nothing that the Israelite could devise was able to effect such a restoration, for no other means could remove the ceremonial uncleanness.

So it is only in the Cross of Christ that a power can be found capable of separating the soul from all moral defilement.

And because such defilement throws the soul out of communion with God, all Christian duties performed in that condition, however scrupulously discharged, are but "dead works," for they have no breath of spiritual life.

As it is our privilege to know that we are reconciled to God by the death of His Son, so it is our privilege to see that by the same atoning death we are separated from the defilement of sin. The source of our pardon and justification is the source also of our purity. And if we know what it is to be freed from the penalty due to our guilt, so we may know what it is to be cleansed and to be kept cleansed, as to our inward consciousness, from all impurity. It is only thus that we can learn what *abiding* fellowship with God really means.

He "gave Himself for us, that He might redeem us from all iniquity" (Titus 2:14). That is, Christ gave Himself as a ransom to redeem us from the enemy's power. Lawlessness is here regarded as the power from whose control we are set free. But this was not the only purpose of His death. "And purify unto Himself a peculiar people," etc. The purification of those He died to redeem is also the aim of His sacrifice. And both blessings are received in the same way.

How many who have grasped the first seem to fail in apprehending the second!

The "ashes" of the red heifer were to be applied to the person defiled. In those ashes we have "the indestructible residue of the entire victim." Those ashes included the blood, after the sacrifice was completed. They were available for the cleansing of the defiled Israelite. The death of the victim was not repeated, for that sacrifice pointed to the death of Christ, which was "once for all." But the ashes were set apart for endless application. The "water of separation," by which the virtue of the sacrifice was applied, was not water alone but water impregnated with the "ashes." The unclean one was sprinkled with the water containing these ashes.

What is the spiritual meaning of this? To what does it point? Not to two sources of spiritual relief, one for pardon, another for cleansing. Whether we look at the water as foreshadowing the Holy Spirit or as referring to the Word, the one central point to which all the lines of typical truth here converge is the blood, or the death, of Christ. Is not this the reasoning in the ninth of Hebrews?

If the Old Testament rite effected the cleansing which had reference to ceremonial defilement, "how much more shall the BLOOD of Christ . . . purge your conscience from dead works to serve the living God?" (Hebrews 9:13–14).

We may insist, as some do, that the water in this type refers to the Holy Scripture. This does not detract from the virtue of the blood. As the water carried the ashes—the ashes that contained the blood, and brought the unclean person in contact with the blood—so now it is the Word that brings us to the blood of Christ. But the Word is not the *fountain* of our cleansing; it is only that which brings us *to* the fountain. There is but one fountain for sin and for uncleanness—the Cross of Christ.

What then do we need in order that we may know the cleansing power of the Cross of Christ? Or, to put it in other words, how may we be separated in heart and mind, in our inner consciousness, from the defiling influence of sin? Only by an apprehension of this blessed fact: that Christ died in order to separate us from sin's defilement.

To be cleansed from any impurity is just to be separated from it. Nothing can separate from sin but the death of Christ. The fact and the purpose of that death are revealed in His Word. To bring us into conformity with that death is the office of the Holy Spirit through the Word. This is to know the liberty of the cleansing power, as well as the freedom brought about by the atoning efficacy of Christ's sacrifice for sin.

It has often been shown that sin is to the soul what disease is to the body. The effect of disease on our physical organism is just a picture of what sin produces on our spiritual nature. Sin as a moral defilement has already been touched upon in connection with leprosy. What we have now more especially to consider is the paralyzing or disabling effect of sin.

It will help us to understand what sin is in this

special aspect, and what it is to be freed from its disorganizing effects, if we look at our Lord's miracles as symbols of spiritual healing, illustrations of what He is now doing upon the souls of men. These miracles were not merely manifestations of divine power. They were "signs" of spiritual truth. They were significant of something far higher than mere physical cures. Nor must we limit our interpretation of them to that of "conversion." In the majority of instances they set forth the blessings to be known and realized by those who are God's children. Disease supposes the existence of life. What is disease but life in an abnormal or morbid condition? Disease has been defined as "any state of the living body in which the natural functions of the organs are interrupted or disturbed." Every cure that our Lord wrought was an emancipation of a part or the whole of the body from such a state of derangement, and represented the liberation of the soul from some particular form of moral evil.

In the eighth chapter of St. Matthew, we have an account of a series of miracles which our Lord wrought immediately after He had preached His Sermon on the Mount. Having unfolded the principles of His kingdom by teaching, He then shows His power by His actions, and communicates His liberating and energizing virtue by healing all their diseases. We have here in this chapter leprosy, paralysis, fever, and other forms of evil; but Christ was able to cure them all.

What did those physical ailments set forth but different aspects of sin as a disease?

In the dysfunction of paralysis we see the loss of the power of voluntary muscular motion. It may be a loss of the power of motion without a loss of sensation, or a loss of sensation without loss of motion, or a loss of both. It appears under different forms. Sometimes it attacks the whole system; or it may affect but one side of the body; and at other times a single member only is affected.

Sin has precisely the same effect on our souls. Though there is spiritual life, there may be lack of spiritual vigor. The effects of sin may be traced in the impairment of voluntary power, in the enfeebling of all moral energy, or in the hardening and deadening of the spiritual sense. And the result is that the whole tone of the spiritual life is lowered. Sin thus robs us of the power by which alone we are able to perform the functions that belong to our renewed being. And it not only undermines our strength, it hinders our growth. The child may have all the parts of its body complete, every organ, every faculty, and yet it will fail to grow if struck down with paralysis. So with the soul. The new birth may have taken place, the great change of conversion to God may have been clear and unmistakable, and yet sin may have been allowed to come in and produce its paralyzing effects. It not only robs us of all spiritual energy, it retards our progress, it hinders our growth.

But disease not only enfeebles and deadens the vital powers; it may bring about positive defects in the bodily organism. Take, for instance, the case of the man born blind, or of the one who was deaf and dumb. Here we see something beyond the mere weakening or paralyzing consequences of disease. So with sin. We may look at it from this point of view—as a privation. This we see in the unregenerate and also in the regenerate. It may so affect the spiritual organs of our moral being that in course of time these organs cease to act. The words "having eyes they see not" become actually fulfilled.

In the case of the deaf mute, what a picture we have of spiritual things! "They bring unto Jesus one that was deaf, and had an impediment in his speech." He was incapable of hearing or of speaking. He was destitute of two of our noblest faculties. The organs were there, but practically the man was as if they were not. Two channels of communication with the outer world were thus closed to him.

How did Jesus effect the cure? What was the order of the deliverance? With which organ did He begin? He first opened the ear. Now the ear we know is an organ of reception. This is its design. It is made for the purpose of receiving, not of giving. It is the channel by which impressions pass into the mind from without.

The man was destitute of the power of receiving sounds. The organ was not absent, but it was disorganized. The doors were closed—the avenue was blocked up. He was insensible to all such impressions.

It is so spiritually. Sin has robbed man of his power of hearing God's voice. And sin will rob the believer, if he yields to it, of the same faculty—hearkening to the voice of the Lord.

To hear is the first act of faith. "Hear, and your soul shall live." "He that heareth My word, and believeth on Him that sent Me, hath everlasting life." And hearkening must go on throughout the whole life.

Then the Lord Jesus loosed his tongue.

The tongue is the instrument of speech. The man was

destitute of the power of communicating his thoughts. It is the faculty by which we tell out what we have realized by taking in. It is the instrument we use when we sing to God's praise, when we give utterance to our gratitude, and when we bear witness before men. It is of all organs the one most required by the messenger who goes forth to proclaim the glad tidings of salvation.

Now all this finds its parallel in the spiritual life.

Sin has robbed man of the power of giving praise to God, or of calling upon Him in prayer. It has deprived him of the ability of testifying to men. It has closed his mouth, it has made him dumb as well as deaf.

Now these two faculties—hearing and speaking— are mutually dependent. When people are born deaf, they usually remain dumb. Hearing is an inborn faculty, but speaking—that is, articulate speech—is an acquired art. Man learns to speak by hearing. But how can he learn if he is born deaf?

So also there is an intimate connection in the spiritual life between the similar faculties of the soul. The ears must be unstopped before the mouth is opened. Effective speaking for God depends upon right hearkening to God. It is by hearkening that the heart is filled. And it is out of the abundance of the heart that the mouth speaks.

Jesus said, "Ephphatha" ("Be opened"). Both the ears and the tongue were set free.

That act was symbolical of the whole of Christ's ministry. He came, not only to redeem the soul, but to liberate every power and faculty we possess, and which God originally created for His glory.

Satan's great aim is to enslave and carry into captivity. He seeks to close every avenue which brings the soul into communion with God. Christ has come to open the prison doors—to burst the fetters that keep the soul in slavery to sin. "The effect of His ministry was one continual Ephphatha"—the emancipation of every moral and spiritual power, the loosening of every chain.

We all acknowledge the power of habit. Experience teaches us that the actions, and especially the oft-repeated actions, of days gone by are a real power in us today. "The present is the resultant of the past." Habit is the power and ability of doing anything acquired by frequent repetition. What at first was difficult, and imperfectly performed, by habit becomes easy, and is executed thoroughly.

Habit, therefore, is an acquired power, and is the result of repeated action. It is often like a second nature.

It is clear from this that we are not born with habits, though we inherit that which gave rise to them. Evil habits must not therefore be confounded with those sinful tendencies with which every child of Adam comes into the world. We are born with the sinful tendency, but we are not born with the sinful habit.

"Man is a bundle of habits." But his conduct is the result of something more than mere habit. Perhaps it would be impossible to exaggerate the power exercised by habit on our daily life. And yet it is of the greatest importance that we should recognize the clear distinction that exists between the inherent tendency and the acquired habit. Every evil habit may be entirely laid aside; we may be completely delivered from the power of any habit. But this does not mean that the tendency to sin is thereby eradicated.

Now there is a very close connection between acquired habits and desires. "If a bad set of habits has grown up with the growth of the individual, or if a single bad tendency be allowed to become a habitual spring of action, a far stronger effort of volition will be required to determine the conduct in opposition to them. This is especially the case when the habitual idea possesses an emotional character, and becomes the source of *desires;* for the more frequently these are yielded to, the more powerful is the solicitation they exert. And the Ego may at last be so completely subjugated by them as scarcely to retain any power of resistance, his will being weakened by the habit of yielding, as the desire gains strength by the habit of acting upon it" (Carpenter's *Mental Physiology*).

Thus we see "by means of habit, passion builds its body, and exercises as well the spiritual as the bodily organs for the service of sin" (Martensen's *Christian Ethics*). "The union of habit and passion is vice, in which a man becomes a bondman to a particular sin. In the language of daily life one is accustomed to designate as vices only those sins that dishonor a man in the eyes of the world, like drunkenness, thieving, unchastity, and the like; as also one understands by an irreproachable, spotless walk in general, merely one that shows no spot on the robe of civil righteousness.

"But why should not one be at liberty to designate as vice every sin that gains such a dominion over the man that he becomes its bondman? Why should not pride, envy, malice, gossip (evil speaking), unmercifulness, not be called vices—that is, when they have gained such a dominion that the man has forfeited his freedom?" (*Ibid.*).

In his Epistle to the Ephesians, St. Paul enumerates a number of sins, all of which may be included under the head of acquired habits (Ephesians 4:25–32). Falsehood, theft, corrupt speech, bitterness, wrath, anger, clamor, railing, malice: all these are to be laid aside— not subjugated or kept under, but altogether put away— as things with which the believer has nothing more to do, and from which he is to be actually separated. "Wherefore putting away"—that is, *stripping off*—all these sins, as one puts off clothes. The very *desire* to yield to them may be removed.

The Apostle Peter, when he presses upon his readers the privilege and duty of holiness, brings them at once to the Cross of Christ. This is his argument: "Be ye holy; for I am holy. . . . Forasmuch as ye know that ye were not redeemed with corruptible things, as silver and gold, from your vain conversation [manner of life] received by tradition from your fathers; but with the precious blood of Christ, as of a lamb without blemish and without spot" (1 Peter 1:16, 18–19).

We may thus claim, as one of the benefits of Christ's death, *complete and immediate deliverance from the evil power of our past manner of life.* Christ died to redeem us from every evil habit of mind and of body— from every false or dishonest course of action—from every vain or untrue line of conduct—from every base or impure motive.

It is sometimes asked by those who entertain the idea that sin can be absolutely eradicated, "How can sin and holiness dwell together in the same heart? How can a man be sick and well at one and the same time? Is he not freed from disease when he is in perfect health? And may it not be said of the soul on whom Christ has laid His healing hand that, being made 'whole,' sin as a disease is entirely removed?"

The inference, therefore, is that all sin—not only as a transgression, but as a principle—is eradicated, when the soul is living up to its true privileges. The "law of sin" then, it is said, no longer exists. The very *tendency* to evil is destroyed.

No one, of course, questions the *possibility* of a Christian's sinning. Even Adam in his original sinless and innocent condition was not free from the *possibility* of sinning. But there are some who seem to think we may be freed in this life from all *tendency* to sin. There are some who seem to maintain that the blessing of being "pure in heart" is a *state* of purity, rather than a *maintained condition* of purity. The distinction is important.

It may be made clear by an illustration. Let us suppose a natural impossibility: namely, that by passing a lighted candle through a dark room, such an effect is produced by that *one act* that the room not only becomes instantly lighted, but *continues* in a *state* of illumination. If this were possible, the room would not be dependent on the continued presence of the lighted candle for its light, though it would be indebted to the candle in the first instance for the state of light introduced into it.

Such is not, we maintain, the nature of the cleansing which Christ bestows upon us.

Adopting the same illustration—but without supposing an impossibility—let the darkness represent sin, and the light holiness. What the lighted candle is to the dark room, Christ is to the heart of the believer.

By the light of His own indwelling presence He keeps sin outside the region of our consciousness. The cleansing thus brought about and realized is not a state but a maintained condition, having no existence whatever apart from Christ Himself.

When a light is introduced into a dark chamber the darkness instantly disappears, but the *tendency* to darkness remains; and the room can only be maintained in a condition of illumination by the continual counteraction of that tendency. The chamber is illuminated by "a continual flow of rays of light, each succeeding pencil of which does not differ from that by which the room was first illuminated."

Here then we have, not a state, but a maintained condition, and an apt illustration of the law of entire and continual dependence.

If it were a state of purity that Christ produced in the soul, then we could conceive of it as having an existence apart from the present activity of His indwelling. And to what would such a notion inevitably lead? To the habit of being occupied with a *state* of purity rather than with Him who is made of God unto us "sanctification." Then the delusion follows as a natural consequence, that we need not depend upon Christ continually for the counteraction of the ever-present tendency to evil, "the law of sin and death."

"We are prone to imagine," writes Professor Drummond, "that nature is full of life. In reality, it is full of death. One cannot say it is natural for a plant to live. Examine its nature fully, and you have to admit that its natural *tendency* is to die. It is kept from dying by a mere temporary endowment, which gives it an ephemeral dominion over the elements—gives it power to utilize for a brief span the rain, the sunshine, and the air. Withdraw this temporary endowment for a moment, and its true nature is revealed. Instead of overcoming nature, it is overcome. The very things which appeared to minister to its growth and beauty now turn against it and make it decay and die. The sun which warmed it withers it; the air and rain which nourished it rot it. It is the very forces which we associate with life which, when their true nature appears, are discovered to be really the ministers of death.

"This law, which is true for the whole plant-world, is also valid for the animal and for man. Air is not life, but corruption—so literally corruption that the only way to keep out corruption, when life has ebbed, is to keep out air. Life is merely a temporary suspension of these destructive powers; and this is truly one of the most accurate definitions of life we have yet received: 'the sum total of the functions which resist death.'

"Spiritual life, in like manner, is the sum total of the functions which resist sin. The soul's atmosphere is the daily trial, circumstance, and temptation of the world. And as it is life alone which gives the plant power to utilize the elements, and as, without it, *they* utilize *it*, so it is the spiritual life alone which gives the soul power to utilize temptation and trial, and without it they destroy the soul" (*Natural Law in the Spiritual World*).

To understand the great principle here set forth is to

grasp the key to the whole question. Here is the solution of the great mystery. How can the tendency to sin exist in the presence of the indwelling Holy Spirit of God? By the law of counteraction. "The law of the Spirit of life in Christ Jesus hath made me free from the law of sin and death" (Romans 8:2). The very fact that the "law of the Spirit of life" is in force, and is ever a continual necessity, is a proof that the law of sin and death is not extinct but is simply counteracted; in other words, that the tendency to sin is still there.

One ignorant of the laws of natural life might conclude that a plant, while manifesting the activity and freshness of vigorous growth, is absolutely free from the influence of those forces which tend to reduce it to a condition of death and decay. In other words, that so long as the plant is in the vigor of life, all tendency to die is destroyed, or nonexistent—that the only power then in operation, in fact, is the power of life. That might be the popular view of the matter. It certainly would not be the real condition of things. Let us not make a similar mistake in the matter of our spiritual condition.

Never in this life are we absolutely free from the presence of evil; the tendency to sin and death is ever with us.

As with the plant, so with the holiest saint: the vital principle has only to be withdrawn for an instant and the natural tendency is at once apparent. Apart from Christ as the indwelling life even the most advanced believer would at once relapse into a state of spiritual decay, because the law of sin would no longer be counteracted.

But, on the other hand, while recognizing the fact that we are not only liable but prone to sin—that we have to the last a downward bias—let us not forget that Christ is stronger than Satan and sin. By His death He has separated us from sin as to its penalty, its service, its defilement, its enfeebling consequences, its habits; and so "in His life," His indwelling life, He sets us free from its *law*. By the law of the Spirit of life He so counteracts the natural tendency to sin that both its tyranny and strain are gone.

Christ's death has for its end our *separation* from the evil. In those five aspects of sin we have here considered, we have endeavored to show that freedom comes through the death of Jesus Christ.

But in this last aspect of sin, it is not absolute separation or eradication that the Scripture puts before us as our present privilege, but counteraction. It is not, therefore, to the death but to the *life* of Christ, His risen life, that we are here directed. The law of the living Christ—that law into which we are introduced when we know what it is to be in vital fellowship with the risen Christ—sets us free and keeps us in a condition of freedom from the law of sin and death.

There is therefore now no condemnation to them which are in Christ Jesus, who walk not after the flesh, but after the Spirit. For the law of the Spirit of life in Christ Jesus hath made me free from the law of sin and death (Romans 8:1–2).

Without Me ye can do nothing (John 15:5).

I can do all things through [in] Christ which strengthened me (Philippians 4:13).

Be strong in the grace that is in Christ Jesus (2 Timothy 2:1).

2

NO CONDEMNATION

TO UNDERSTAND the full meaning of the privilege "no condemnation" we must know what is meant by the term "in Christ Jesus." The phrase "in Christ" is almost peculiar to St. Paul. It occurs in his epistles alone about seventy-eight times. But the germ is found in the words of our Lord: "Abide in Me, and I in you" (John 15:4).

A careful examination of the various passages will show us that the truth expressed in the words "in Christ" has two distinct aspects—the one referring to justification, the other to sanctification. While we would distinguish one from the other, we would not separate them. There is what we may term the "in Christ" of standing, and the "in Christ" of walk or experience. The former has reference to headship, the latter to fellowship.

Headship. Each of us occupies one of two positions—Adam or Christ. God's dealings have reference to two men—the first and the last Adam. The whole human race was headed up in Adam. We must not regard humanity as so many separate individuals—like a heap of sand—but as an organic unity—like a tree;

though consisting of an innumerable number of parts, yet forming one whole. In Adam, then, we see the whole family of man summed up; and there, in him, we see the whole race on its trial.

Adam's trial was man's probation. It was not the trial of a single individual, it was the trial of the whole human race. All were included in him. His fall was the fall of the whole family. "Through one man sin entered into the world, and death through sin; and so death passed unto all men, for that all sinned" (Romans 5:12, ASV). ["All sinned" (aorist), that is, in Adam. Probation may be looked at either as having reference to salvation or to service. Probation so far as salvation is concerned is no longer a question of our own works. In that sense our probation terminated with Adam's failure. But probation in connection with service is still going on. And it is in that sense that we must understand the apostle as writing when he says, ". . . lest that by any means, when I have preached to others, I myself should be a castaway," or "should be rejected" (ASV)—(1 Corinthians 9:27)—disproved or rejected, that is, as to service.]

There we have the end of the trial. The Fall terminates, strictly speaking, human probation.

It is to such that the gospel comes. Not to those whose trial is undecided, who are in process of being tested, who are still on probation; but to those whose opportunity on that ground is forever gone—to those, therefore, who are "lost."

And what does the gospel propose? Does it come proposing another trial? Does it come offering to put man on a second probation? Nothing of the sort. The burden of its message is not probation but redemption.

Take an illustration. Here is a tree with numerous branches. Cut the root, and what happens? Death; it not only enters into the stem, it passes over the whole tree, it affects each branch and every leaf.

To propose the improvement of the old position in Adam is like the vain effort of endeavoring to revive the life in the separate branches of the dead tree.

The gospel proclaims a new creation: a new tree—union with a new root—being grafted on to a new stock. "If any man be in Christ, he is a new creature" (2 Corinthians 5:17). This is not to improve the old, but to be translated into a new position.

Take another illustration. Here is a man, let us suppose, who has failed in business. He is not only hopelessly insolvent; his credit is gone, and his name is disgraced. All efforts of his own to retrieve his position are utterly fruitless; he is beyond all hope of recovery in that direction. But hope comes to him from another quarter. Let us suppose he is taken into partnership by one whose name stands high in the commercial world. He becomes a partner in a wealthy and honorable firm. All his debts are paid by that firm, and the past is canceled. But this is not all. He gets an entirely new standing. His old name is set aside, forgotten, buried forever. He has now a new name. In that name he transacts all his business. His old name is never again mentioned.

We have here a faint shadow of what the gospel bestows. To be a believer in Christ is to have passed out of our old position —to lose our old name—and to take our stand on an entirely new ground. We are baptized "into the name of the Lord"; we are "in Christ."

"There is therefore now no condemnation to them which are *in Christ Jesus.*" This is not a privilege that comes to the believer by degrees; it is complete and absolute at once. And the moment the transition takes place the believer stands, not on the ground of probation, but on the ground of redemption.

This truth is fundamental. The "in Christ" of standing is the foundation of all practical godliness, of all Christian service. We must start here or we cannot take a single step in the way of holiness.

But this does not exhaust the meaning of the phrase "in Christ"; nor is this all that is to be understood by the apostle's declaration in the opening words of this eighth chapter of his Epistle to the Romans. Included in this statement is also the thought of—

Fellowship. To be "in Christ" in this sense is to have the consciousness of His favor. This is a matter not of standing, but of experience—and yet not of feeling, but of faith. We are commanded to "abide" in Christ. But that which has reference to our judicial standing cannot be a matter of exhortation. Those who have taken their stand in Christ—who are justified—are now required to remain, to dwell, or abide in Him for *sanctification.* The "in Christ" which has to do with our experience and walk, which relates to our sanctification, is constantly a matter of exhortation in the Scriptures.

It is possible, alas! not to abide in Him. And what happens when the believer ceases to abide? He then lives the self-life. There is such a thing as a religious self-life. Is it not the life that is too often manifested even by those who have a saving knowledge of Christ? There may be a clear apprehending of what it is to be "in Christ" as to justification, and yet much darkness and perplexity as to the "in Christ" of sanctification. Many have a true aim, seeking to glorify Christ and to be made like Him—they have sincere and earnest desires, and they are making constant and vigorous efforts after holiness—and yet they are continually being disappointed. Failure and defeat meet them at every turn. Not because they do not try, not because they do not struggle—they do all this—but because the life they are living is essentially the *self-life* and not the *Christ-life*.

They are brought into condemnation. This arises from the fact that the "law of sin" in their members is stronger than their renewed nature.

The soul that ceases to abide in Christ lives the "I myself" life. The words *"them which are in Christ Jesus"* (in Romans 8:1), form a contrast to the expression *"I as I am in myself,"* the theme of the last verses of chapter 7 (Godet).

"I myself"—"apart from and in opposition to the help which I derive from Christ" (*N.T. Commentary*, edited by Bishop Ellicott)—I myself am conscious of a miserable condition of internal conflict, between two opposite tendencies—the two natures: the one consenting to the law that it is good, delighting in it, and desiring to fulfill its requirements; the other drawing me in the contrary direction, and, being the more powerful of the two, actually bringing me into captivity to the law of sin, and thus resulting in a condition of condemnation.

"I in myself." "This expression is the key to the whole passage (Romans 7:14–25). St. Paul, from verses 14 to 24, has been speaking of himself as he was *in himself*" (Conybeare and Howson).

"There is therefore now no condemnation." "This word *no* (*aucune*)," as Professor Frederic Louis Godet, writing in French, observes, "shows that there is more than one sort of condemnation resting on the head of him who is not in Christ Jesus. There is, first, the divine displeasure excited by the violation of the law—the anger described in the first three chapters of the Epistle to the Romans. The two following chapters represent to us the removal of this condemnation by the blood of Christ, and by the faith that consents to come and draws its pardon thence.

"But if, after this, sin continues the master of the soul, condemnation will infallibly revive. For Jesus did not come to save us *in* sin, but *from* sin. It is not pardon which constitutes the health of the soul; it is salvation, it is the restoration of holiness. The reception of pardon does not affect our resemblance to God; holiness alone does this. Pardon is the threshold of salvation, the means by which convalescence is begun. Health itself is holiness.

"If, then, the first condemnation to be taken away is that of sin as a *fault*, the second, which must necessarily be removed too in order that the first may not return, is sin as a *power*, as the inwrought tendency of the will. And it is the removal of this second condemnation that St. Paul here describes: 'the law of the Spirit of life in Christ Jesus hath made me free from the law of sin and death' (Romans 8:2)."

In this "I myself" life the evil tendency gains the ascendency. So that, though with the new nature—the inner man or spiritual mind—we serve the law of God, yet we are nevertheless overcome and are practically brought into captivity to the law of sin. Such a life must of necessity be a life of condemnation in the daily experience.

But another characteristic belongs to this self-life. It is essentially carnal (*sarkinos*) (Romans 7:14. See Appendix, Note B), though not carnal in the sense of being unregenerate. A carnal man may be also one who has been born of the Spirit but is not sufficiently actuated by His enlightening and sanctifying power to overcome the hostile power of the flesh; he still thinks, feels, judges, acts, "according to the flesh" (Lange's *Commentary* on 1 Corinthians 3:1).

The condition described by "carnal" may be either the immature stage of the young convert or a state of relapse into which the more advanced believer has fallen. To the *first* no blame can be attached, for all must pass through this stage in their progress from the natural to the spiritual. But to the *second* condemnation belongs, as we see from the way in which the apostle writes to the Corinthian believers: "I could not speak unto you as unto spiritual, but as unto carnal, even as unto babes in Christ" (1 Corinthians 3:1).

"He is here not speaking of Christians as distinguished from the world, but of one class of Christians as distinguished from another" (Hodge).

This is the description of every believer, even an apostle, regarded *as he is in himself*. And such is the *experience* of the believer when he lives out of fellowship with Christ. The carnal or fleshly principle gains the ascendancy. He is no longer spirit, soul and body, but rather body, soul and spirit, the order being reversed, the lowest principle becoming dominant.

To be "in Christ" as to fellowship is to have the individual human spirit apprehended, or laid hold of, by the Holy Spirit of God. We are thus not only brought into harmony with God but linked with the power of God. The ability we lack when we struggle to overcome in the self-life is no longer lacking in the Christ-life. This is to be free from the law of sin and death—this is to be spiritually minded.

The following remarks by an able and distinguished theologian are well worthy of careful perusal. "We maintain now, as ever, that even in Romans 7:14–24, Paul is speaking 'out of the consciousness of the regenerate person,' without thereby meaning to say that he is giving utterance to experiences which are permitted to the regenerate as such—rather, experiences which even the regenerate person is not spared. It certainly appears an irreconcilable contradiction to say that one and the same man is fleshly, sold unto sin (chap. 7:14), and yet, on the other hand, is free from the law of sin and death by the Spirit of life that is in Christ Jesus (chap. 8:2).

"But the apostle actually places the two states in juxtaposition, as belonging to his present condition. He does not say in 7:14 that he was *previously* consisting of fleshly material and *was* sold under sin, but that this is his *natural* constitution, and that this contrariety *subsists* between him and God's spiritual law. *He speaks in the present;* and when he sets forth, in continuation, that his acknowledgement of the law does not help him to do the prescribed good, but that sin, in spite of his own will, makes him do that which is against God's will, he speaks throughout in the *present.*

"This established present claims to be all the more considered, that the apostle (chap. 7:7–13) *also actually speaks in historical form of a fact of experience which at that time belongs to the past*. He looks back there into his childhood, and shows how, in the degree that the claim of law entered into his consciousness, the sin which was present in him, but not present as his personal conduct, became his personal sin, and the cause of his self-incurred death. It was the saving purpose of the law declared in verse 13 which he thus painfully experienced. From verse 14 onwards, the apostle then depicts how he, the self-consciously willing one, finds himself and his doing disposed in the light of the law. Every Christian is compelled to confirm what the apostle here says, from his own personal experience. And well for him if he can also confirm the fact that God's law, and therefore God's will, is his delight—that he desires the good and hates the evil; and, indeed, in such a way that the sin to which, against his will, he is hurried away, *is foreign to his inmost nature*. But woe to him if from his own personal experience he could only confirm *this*, and not *also* the fact that the Spirit of the new life that has its source in Christ Jesus *has freed him from the urgency of sin, and the condition of death*, which were not abrogated through the law but only brought to light; *so that his will*, which by the law was inclined towards what is good, even though powerless, *but now actually capable of good, is opposed* (*as a predominating, overmastering power of life which will finally triumph in glory*) to the death that continues to work in him" (Delitzsch, *System of Biblical Psychology*, pp. 453–455).

But it has been objected, "If I am in Christ, and am depicting that which I am out of Christ, I depict *in concreto*, not what I actually am, but what I once was out of Christ" (Philippi).

Now, as Delitzsch observes, it is only necessary to look into one's own heart to see at once what a sophism this is. Every man who is in Christ knows from actual experience what it is to be out of Christ in his walk and life. Every believer knows from sad experience what it is to cease to abide in Christ. Not that it is possible to live both lives at one and the same time—that is, to be in Christ as to fellowship and out of Christ in the same sense, at any one moment. The objection urged is based upon the assumption that the term "in Christ" can be understood only in one sense. But the twofold sense of the phrase, or the double aspect of the truth, is what we have endeavored to elucidate.

It is the believer's privilege to know that there is now no condemnation for him, whether he thinks of himself as standing before God as a Judge or as walking before God as a Father. In the first case he stands before God enveloped in Christ the Righteous One, who has met all the claims of the righteous law; in the other, he is abiding in Christ the Holy One, who has satisfied all the desires of a Father's heart.

Thus walking, he knows the blessedness of pleasing God. Surely it is to this condition of soul that the apostle refers when he says, "Beloved, if our heart condemn us not" (1 John 3:21)—not if we stand justified in Christ, but if our heart be not accusing us—"we have confidence toward God."

It is worthy of note that while the Apostle Paul in

those eleven verses (Romans 7:14–24) refers to himself, either directly or indirectly, some thirty times, he does not there make a single reference either to Christ or the Holy Spirit. In reading that passage it is not necessary to suppose that the apostle is speaking from the standpoint of a present *experience*, but from the standpoint of a present *conviction*, as to the *tendencies* of the two natures that were then and there present within him.

The freedom of which the apostle speaks in the opening words of the eighth chapter, he enforces by an *inference* and a *reason*. The inference or conclusion is indicated by the word "therefore." "There is therefore now," etc. But to what point in the argument does this note of inference refer? To what does it go back? A careful perusal shows us that this first verse is a conclusion springing out of the first six verses of the seventh chapter.

Three great truths he had put before his readers: substitution, identification, and union. The thought of substitution he unfolds in chapter 5: "Christ died *for* the ungodly," "Christ died *for* us," verses 6 and 8 (see Appendix, Note A). Here, too, we have the headship of the first and second representatives, Adam and Christ, dwelt upon.

The thought of identification he brings out in chapter 6. The believer is there regarded as crucified and buried *with* Christ. See verses 6 and 4. And then there is the thought of union. It is in the opening portion of chapter 7 that this truth is set forth. "Ye are become dead to the law by the body of Christ, that ye should be *married* to another." This truth is dwelt on only in the first six verses. At the seventh verse a digression begins, and the subject of union is not again taken up until the first verse of chapter 8. The progress of thought in these three great facts—substitution, identification, and union—is indicated in the prepositions "for," "with," and "in." It has been said with truth, an immense amount of theology is contained in the prepositions of the New Testament.

"Therefore now *in* Christ Jesus"—being brought into union with Him, not only judicially but experientially also—"there is no condemnation."

But the apostle assigns a reason for this blessed state of things, in these words: "For the law of the Spirit of life in Christ Jesus hath made me free from the law of sin and death." By this union we are brought into a condition of deliverance. We get the benefit of a liberating power. Redemption then is realized to be an emancipation from sin, not merely by virtue of an act done in the past but by virtue of a law which is in force in the present—of a law which never ceases to be in force. One law is, in fact, being effectually counteracted by another law. Fellowship with Christ, union of heart and mind with Him, introduces the person into that sphere where all the benefits of this victorious law become his. It is there, "in Christ Jesus," and *only* there, that this blessed freedom can be known and realized.

What we are *out* of that sphere we see mirrored in those eleven verses in chapter 7; but what we are *in* Him—within the circle of His presence—we learn from chapter 8.

The believer is thus reminded of the truth of that terse but pregnant sentence spoken by the Lord Himself: "Without Me," or apart from Me, "ye can do nothing" (John 15:5); that is, without fellowship with Me, even after you have been brought to know Me as your Lord and Savior. "It is a poor and inadequate interpretation of the words 'without Me' to make them to mean 'Ye can do nothing *until* ye are in Me, and have My grace.' It is rather, '*After* ye are in Me, ye can even then accomplish nothing, except ye draw life and strength from Me. . . . From first to last it is I that must work in and through you'" (Trench).

If a piece of iron could speak, what could it say of itself? "I am black; I am cold; I am hard." But put it in the furnace, and what a change takes place! It has not ceased to be iron; but the blackness is gone, and the coldness is gone, and the hardness is gone! It has entered into a new experience. The fire and the iron are still distinct, and yet how complete is the union—they are one. If the iron could speak, it could not glory in itself, but in the fire that makes and keeps it a bright and glowing mass. So must it be with the believer. Do you ask him what he is in himself? He answers, "*I* am carnal, sold under sin." For, left to himself, this inevitably follows; he is brought into captivity to the law of sin which is in his members. But it is his privilege to enter into fellowship with Christ, and in Him to abide. And there, *in Him*, who is our life, our purity, and our power—in Him, whose Spirit can penetrate into every part of our being—the believer is no longer carnal, but spiritual; no longer overcome by sin and brought into captivity, but set free from the law of sin and death and preserved in a condition of deliverance. This blessed experience of emancipation from sin's service and power implies a momentary and continuous act of abiding.

The believer cannot glory in himself. He cannot glory in a state of purity attained, and having an existence apart from Christ Himself. He is like the piece of iron. The moment it is withdrawn from the furnace, the coldness and hardness and blackness begin to return. It is not by a work wrought in the iron once for all but by the momentary and continual influence of the fire on the iron that its tendency to return to its natural condition is counteracted.

Such is the law of liberty in the spiritual life. We can thus understand how there may be a continuous experience of deliverance from the law of sin and at the same time a deepening sense of our own natural depravity—a life of triumph over evil with a spirit of the truest humility.

The following is an extract from Bishop Ellicott's *New Testament Commentary for English Readers*, on the opening words of Romans 8:

> It differs from the first section of chapter 5 in this, that while both describe the condition of the regenerate Christian, and both cover the whole range of time from the first admission to the Christian communion down to the ultimate and assured enjoyment of Christian immortality, chapter 5 lays stress chiefly on the initial and final moments of this period, whereas chapter 8 emphasizes rather the whole intermediate process. In technical language, the one turns chiefly upon justification, the other upon sanctification.

Dr. Lange, on the same passage, remarks in his commentary:

> The question of the reference to justification or sanctification must affect the interpretation of *condemnation*, since verse

2, beginning with *gar*, seems to introduce a proof. The position of the chapter in the epistle, as well as a fair exegesis of the verses, sustains the reference to sanctification. (Not to the entire exclusion of the other any more than they are sundered in Christian experience.) We must then take *no condemnation* in a wide sense.

That which is born of the Spirit is spirit (John 3:6).

And every thing shall live whither the river cometh (Ezekiel 47:9).

To be spiritually minded is life (Romans 8:6).

Christ liveth in me (Galatians 2:20).

The water that I shall give him shall be in him a well of water springing up into everlasting life (John 4:14).

He that believeth on Me, as the scripture hath said, out of his belly shall flow rivers of living water (John 7:38).

3

LIFE

A REMARKABLE brick from the wall of Babylon bears the inscription of one of its mighty kings. It was the custom to imprint the royal mark upon the bricks used for public works. In the center of this inscription is a footprint of one of the dogs which wandered about the crowded city. While this particular brick was lying in its plastic state to dry, a vagrant dog had accidentially trodden upon it. The king's inscription is entirely illegible, while the footprint of the dog is perfectly distinct. The name of the mighty ruler of Babylon is unknown. The footprint of the dog has decidedly the advantage over the inscription of the king (Norton).

May we not see a picture here of man's present condition? Created originally "in the image and after the likeness of God," man, as he is now by nature, no longer reflects the moral beauty and perfection of the divine character. While in one part of his nature—the soul—God's image is defaced, in another part—the spirit—it is altogether obliterated. The footprint of the evil one is distinctly visible.

And yet we would not say that there are no traces of the original inscription. The Scriptures recognize such outlines, faint though they be, even among the heathen (Romans 2:14–15). And yet, while this is true, the Word of God speaks of man as wholly corrupt, and needing a change so complete and thorough that it is called a "new creation." He "must be born again."

Man as originally created consisted of spirit, soul, and body. We read, "The LORD God formed man of the dust of the ground, and breathed into his nostrils the breath of life; and man became a living soul" (Genesis 2:7).

In order of thought, we have first the construction of the body. Man was made of the dust of the ground and fashioned by the hand of God, as the potter fashions the clay. Then, into that body thus formed, God breathed "the breath of life." And yet "the formation of man from the dust and the breathing of the breath of life must not be understood in a mechanical sense as if God first of all constructed a human figure from the dust and then, by breathing His breath of life into the clod of earth which He had shaped into the form of man, made it into a living being. . . . By an act of divine omnipotence man arose from the dust; and in the same moment in which the dust, by virtue of creative omnipotence, shaped itself into a human form, it was pervaded by the divine breath of life and created a living being, so that we cannot say the body was earlier than the soul" (Delitzsch).

"Man became a *living soul*." Though the same term, *nephesh chay*, is employed to designate the lower animals (Genesis 1:21, 24 and 2:19), "it does not necessarily imply that the basis of the life-principle in man and the inferior animals is the same. The distinction between the two appears from the difference in the mode of their creations. The beasts arose as the Almighty issued creative commands to the earth—arose as completed beings, every one a living soul. Man, however, received his life from a distinct act of divine in-breathing—a communication from the whole Personality of the Godhead. In effect, man was thereby constituted a living soul like the lower animals; but in him the life-principle conferred a *personality* which was wanting in them" (Delitzsch).

Man received not only that part which we term soul but also that part termed spirit. He was not a mere individual creature, like the lower animals: he became a *person*. That personality was the meeting point of the two natures, the animal and the spiritual. He consisted, therefore, of the three parts—spirit, soul, and body. Body and spirit uniting in the personal soul is the true idea of man as he came forth from the hand of God.

But what is man's present constitution since the Fall? The Scriptures declare that he is now by nature "dead in trespasses and sin." That is, so far as his spirit-nature is concerned, towards God he is dead. Not, we would observe, that his spirit nature has ceased to exist. Not that, since the Fall, he has become body and soul, instead of body, soul, and spirit. For while he is dead towards God, he is not dead towards sin.

But what then about Jude 19: ". . . sensual, having not the Spirit"? Even though, with DeWette and others, we may hesitate to accept the interpretation that the reference here is to the Holy Spirit, this passage cannot be pressed as proving that fallen man has ceased to possess a spirit-nature. Dean Alford observes on this text: "These men have not indeed ceased to have *pneuma*, as part of their own tripartite nature; but they have ceased to possess it in any worthy sense: it is degraded beneath and under the power of the *psuche*, the personal life, so as to have no real vitality of its own." The *pneuma* "is that which essentially distinguishes man from an animal, a breath from (out of) God, the noblest part of our nature; but as, in the case of all natural men, it lies concealed, since the Fall, in carnal and animal life, it may be so effectually sunk and buried under the flesh by continual sins *as if* it were no longer extant" (Lange, *Commentary on St. Jude*. See Appendix, Note C). All capacity to understand the things of the Spirit is gone. The Fall has robbed him of the ability to hold communion with God.

And yet fallen man is capable of every kind of sin— not only of sin that pertains to the body and soul, but of sin that pertains to the spirit. He is capable of "*spiritual* wickedness." He must therefore still possess a spirit-nature.

Satan needs the spirit of a man to produce the highest development of human evil.

When therefore it is said that man is dead spiritually, we understand by this that he is utterly incapable of fellowship with God. In this condition of death he is incapable of attaining the true ideal of human nature.

What, then, is man in this state? How do the Scriptures designate him? He is described as "natural." "The natural man receiveth not the things of the Spirit of God" (1 Corinthians 2:14). He is soulish. This is the highest condition he is capable of attaining. He is one whose highest nature is the soul. The natural man is the *soulish* man. He is governed by his soul. He cannot rise higher, but he may sink lower. He may become devilish. His spirit-nature may become satanically possessed.

The natural man is not necessarily one who is the slave of his carnal appetites. He may be a moralist of the highest type. He may be a giant in intellect, as some of the Greek philosophers were, having all that can be derived from the first Adam: one endowed with a rational soul, and who has the use of all his rational faculties, and yet is destitute of the capacity of understanding the things of the Spirit of God or of holding communion with Him.

The reason for this incapacity is clear. The Scripture furnishes the answer: "Because they [God's revelations] are spiritually discerned." From the very nature of the case it must be so. It is not that the natural man *will* not "know" the things of the Spirit—he *cannot* know them.

To put the matter clearly, we may say there are three great spheres—of sense, of reason, and of spirit.

There are the things which come within the sphere of *sense*. The lower animals are endowed with the faculties of seeing and knowing these things in common with man. They can touch and taste and see. These powers are possessed by the brute creation as well as by ourselves. We convince ourselves of the substantial reality of the material world by these faculties of sense.

Then there are the things which come within the sphere of *reason*. Now we rise into a higher domain— into a region which is beyond the reach of the lower animals. Man alone has the power of drawing deductions, forming conclusions, and grasping abstract notions. Man alone has the sense of moral obligation.* And lastly, there are the things which come within the sphere of *spirit*. And these the Scripture declares are beyond the reach even of the "natural man"—the psychical or soulish man. These belong to the spirit-life, and are grasped by faith.

You may put a telescope into the hands of a man who is blind and bid him look at some distant star, or on some lovely landscape. He tells you he sees nothing. Well, his witness is true. So the agnostic affirms of all supernatural religion, that he knows it not. His witness also is true. But if the blind man goes further, and asserts that because he sees nothing there is *nothing to see*, his assertion is untrue, and his witness is worthless, because he speaks beyond the range of his capacity.

Such is the value of the natural man's *opinion* when he declares his mind on spiritual things.

---

* In the light of recent experiments with animal behavior, e.g., apes being taught to communicate with humans or each other through sign language, it appears that in the three great spheres mentioned earlier, of sense, of reason, and of spirit, there is some leakage. Animals have been observed to do things that seem to exhibit characteristics of reason, even of spirit, such as ability to communicate, to show great pleasure, shame, to respond in an unexpected but apparently logical fashion—and we tend to call these responses by the same name that we use when humans do them. But these capacities are rigidly circumscribed; no group of animals has ever established a series of training sessions to perpetuate and develop among themselves these capacities and bring them into refinement. Animals clearly have no full access into the spheres of reason and of spirit with respect to a voluntary response to the moving of the Spirit of God, as does man. (Footnote added in 1991.)

But the natural man may *become* spiritual. The spiritually blind may be restored to sight. The agnostic who "knows not" may be brought to see and understand and know.

The life of the spirit-nature may be restored. This is brought about by the operation of the Spirit of God. But how? What is the nature of the process?

Not by the growth of the soul-principle, the development of the natural man. No one passes from the natural sphere into the spiritual by virtue of powers lying dormant in the soul. It is not by the culture of the natural faculties, nor is it by any supposed uncovering of the spirit-nature, as if it only lay buried underneath.

The spirit is quickened by a direct communication of life from above. "That which is born of the flesh is flesh, and that which is born of the Spirit is spirit." "Ye must be born from above."

So to be alive unto God is to have received this divine quickening. "Now we have received, not the spirit of the world, but the Spirit which is of God" (1 Corinthians 2:12).

It is in that spirit-nature the Holy Spirit dwells. Until that nature is quickened there can be no spiritual nourishment, no spiritual instruction or spiritual training. For what is there to feed? What is there to instruct? What is there to develop?

But divine life having been imparted, that which follows is the growth and development of the spirit-principle; and this involves the progressive transformation of the character.

Let us now consider the nature of this transformation.

There is not a more wonderful or comforting thought in the whole Bible than this—that if we are the children of God we are "predestinated to be conformed to the image of His Son." In its *fullest* sense its realization cannot yet take place. It is at His appearing that that likeness will be complete. "We shall be like Him, for we shall see Him as He is."

But this conformity does not belong to the future alone. In a very true sense it is to take place now. It is a change that goes on progressively after divine life has entered into the soul. We are "being changed"—transfigured—"into the same image from glory to glory" (2 Corinthians 3:18).

It is not a mere superficial likeness, as a gold sovereign bears the image of the Queen. That image is put upon it to give the coin currency; but the sovereign is not the image of the Queen, it is simply stamped with it.

It is a change that takes place *from within*. Beginning with the spirit of the man, it advances progressively through every part of his nature. This conformity to the image of God's Son consists of a change of character. Character is not something that is formed at once. It needs time and discipline, and the exercise of the will in the act of choosing, to form character.

Character is the result of conduct. Conduct is the outcome of condition. Right conduct is the fruit of right condition. But before there can be the right condition, there must be the right nature, or constitution. We have thus these four elements in spiritual progress.

The first is *constitution*. There must be a new nature. "And you hath He quickened, who were dead in trespasses and sins" (Ephesians 2:1). In the case of every believer this quickening has taken place.

The apostle could thank God that this was true of all Colossian converts: "Giving thanks unto the Father, who hath made us meet [*hikanos*: precisely adapted, or competent] to be partakers of the inheritance of the saints in light" (Colossians 1:12). Not that they were "precisely adapted" or "made competent" by *progressive growth in holiness*. Such is not the thought. "Who made us competent" (Bishop Lightfoot)—competent to *inherit*. Now, who is it that is competent to inherit an estate? Ask some wealthy landowner how he came into his property, and perhaps he will tell you he purchased it. Ask some of the earth's great men who have rendered signal services to their country how they became possessed of their estates, and perhaps their answer would be that they received them as the reward of their services. They did not *inherit* their possessions.

Only an heir can inherit. But what constitutes an heir? Not talents or education; not personal efforts or great learning. There is only one way by which he becomes an heir. He must be *born* an heir. It is by birth.

So believers are competent to inherit because they have been born into the family of God. We have become, by virtue of that birth, "heirs of God and joint heirs with Christ."

It is for this that the apostle gives thanks. They were meet—that is, competent—to be partakers of the inheritance of the saints in light. They had the new nature. If that is lacking there can be no advance, not a single step in the way of progress can be taken; it is vain to insist on right conduct, or to urge the importance of developing Christian character.

But now we come to *condition*. A spiritual nature is one thing, a spiritual mind is another. Every Christian possesses that which is born of the Spirit; but is every Christian spiritually minded?

Three passages we may look at in which we have the phrase "the mind of Christ" referred to in deeply important connections.

"Let this mind be in you, which was also in Christ Jesus" (Philippians 2:5). Here we have a condition of mind considered in connection with *self*. It was a mind that utterly ignored self. "He emptied Himself." It was on these lines of utter self-abnegation that He glorified His Father. He tells us distinctly, "I can of Mine own self do nothing" (John 5:30); that is, I am not able to be doing a single thing *from* Myself. Again, "I do nothing of Myself" (John 8:28); or, "I *from* Myself am doing nothing." "I speak not of—or *from*—Myself" (John 14:10). He took the place of a servant—of a son. The very idea of sonship involves that of dependence. "Perfect sonship involves perfect identity of will and action with the Father. . . . 'The Father that dwelleth in Me, He doeth the works' (John 14:10). According to the true reading, The Father abiding in Me doeth His work" (Canon Westcott).

Now, the believer is called to walk as Christ walked. This mind of complete self-renunciation, therefore, is the condition to be maintained. "Let this mind be in you." As he lived in and on the Father, so are we to live in and on Christ.

When we are in the right condition, Christ, not self, occupies the center of our being. Then it is that He reigns with unhindered sway as king within. The writer, not long since, heard one who had been a Christian many years describe the nature of the blessing he had recently in the following words: "I had heard of Christ being king. Well, He had reigned in me; but it was only as a constitutional sovereign. *I was prime minister*, and I did a good deal of the work myself. Then I found that *He must be absolute monarch*. And so now He is." How much is involved in that thought! How much turns upon this condition of things! In one sense everything depends upon it.

> Higher than the highest heavens,
>   Deeper than the deepest sea,
> Lord, Thy love at last hath conquered;
> Grant me now my soul's desire:
>   "None of self, and all of Thee."

> PASTOR THEODORE MONOD.

Another passage: "But we have the mind of Christ" (1 Corinthians 2:16). The apostle had referred to the gospel, or the truths of revelation, as the wisdom of God, and as the things of the Spirit. He declares that these things cannot be known apart from the Spirit of God. But then he reminds his readers that they had received the Spirit of God, and this in order that they might know these things. The natural, or unregenerate, man cannot know them. It is the spiritual man alone who is able to discern them. To have "the mind of Christ" is to be spiritually minded.

But it is possible for even the regenerate to become unspiritual; not the "natural man" alone, but even the believer may be without "the mind of Christ." He may become, as the apostle declared these Corinthian Christians had become, "carnal," fleshly—mere "babes"

—no longer capable of spiritual discernment (1 Corinthians 3:1. See Appendix, Note B).

"The mind of Christ" is the essential condition of all spiritual perception, of all progress in divine knowledge. Here is the secret of apprehending the "unsearchable riches of Christ" as they are revealed to us in the Scriptures. We cease to become spiritually intelligent, or receptive of divine teaching, when we cease to possess this condition of mind.

And the same thing applies in the matter of daily guidance. "The mind of Christ" is necessary for a quick understanding of God's will in the hourly events of life.

"There are thousands of points in our journey which require quick and almost instantaneous decision as to what we believe we ought to do. The juncture, perhaps, is such that gives very little space to go to some friend, or even to the divine oracles of truth, or even to ponder the matter in our own breast. At such moments, a rapid perception of the right is an inestimable gift.

"Now those who have been familiar with holy things attain, gradually, to a surprising initiation of what is the mind and will of God on any subject. It is a kind of second spiritual sense. We can scarcely explain to you the process, but the conclusion it brings them to is generally a correct one, and is often far better than any outward weighing or deliberation would have given them. . . . Their first thoughts are better than second thoughts, because in their first thoughts there is less of man and there is more of the Spirit.

"And who are those whose first thoughts are thus to be depended upon? Those who, by continual and long intercourse with the Fountain of love and wisdom, so see an object from His point of view and so measure it by His standard and so feel His affections that they can say, 'We have the mind of Christ'" (Rev. James Vaughan, of Brighton).

While, then, we insist on the necessity of regeneration—the communication of a new *nature*—before there can be the spiritual *mind*, let us not forget that a man may relapse into a wordly condition, though he has become a new creature. He may become "carnally minded." He may *de*-generate, though he cannot become *un*-regenerate. He may cease to mind the things of the Spirit; he may be minding the things of the flesh (Romans 8:5–6). Let us not read those verses in the eighth of Romans as if they had no reference to those who *have* become new creatures in Christ Jesus. They point to a condition of heart and mind into which, alas! many of God's children too frequently fall. And with what result? The loss of all spiritual liberty and power. Liberty is found in obeying the law of one's being. As partakers of the divine nature, we need continually to abide, if we would be free, in the condition which corresponds to the divine nature.

One more passage: "Forasmuch then as Christ hath suffered for us in the flesh, arm yourselves likewise with the same mind: for he that hath suffered in the flesh hath ceased from sin; that he no longer should live the rest of his time in the flesh to the lusts of men, but to the will of God" (1 Peter 4:1–2).

"Arm yourselves with the same mind"—a condition of holy separation from all sin. We have to put on the mind of Him who *has* suffered for sin. The point to be noted here is that it is not so much the mind of Christ as

He was dying, but the mind of Christ who "*hath* suffered for us in the flesh"—referring to His life-sufferings. And the reason follows: "Because He that *hath* suffered as to the flesh hath rest from sin" (Lange, *Commentary*, in loco). "Hence he who puts on His mind, and is in communion with Him, henceforth must serve sin no more" (*Ibid.*).

"The mind of Christ" becomes thus our shield against the power of temptation.

All this is intimately connected with our next point.

Conduct. It will be at once understood why it is that duty is often not only so difficult but so irksome. The difficulty or unpleasantness frequently arises from the absence of right condition.

"If ye be *willing* and obedient." Note the order of the two things. Willingness is a condition of oneness with the divine mind. Conduct breaks down when the harmony is absent, when the fellowship ceases, and the power no longer flows.

Conduct is simply the will in action. The walk that glorifies God, and keeps us in His smile, is the activity of a will that is one with God's will.

Liberty is not freedom *from* law—that would be license. It is freedom *in* law.

There is so-called liberty which is without law. This may be natural man's ideal of true freedom. But "lawlessness" is in God's judgment the very essence of sin.

There is also a condition which is *under* law; but this is a state of bondage, the condition of the legalist.

A third and blessed relation in which we may be to the law is that of being *inlawed*, having it within us, written by the Spirit of God on the fleshly tablets of the heart.

Liberty is not being without control, nor being under coercion; nor is it, strictly speaking, being in a state of self-control. It is to be within the sphere of divine control, having the Spirit of life within and around us.

The Holy Spirit who communicates the nature also produces the condition, and from the condition brings forth the conduct. This is seen in "the fruit of the Spirit" (Galatians 5:22). First, we have a condition of mind produced within us: "love, joy, peace." This state of inward conscious blessing must be brought about preliminary to all outward, practical obedience. Where the Holy Spirit is dwelling without being grieved—as the Comforter rather than as the Reprover—this is the first part of His fruit we are permitted to taste. The believer will know to a greater or less degree what it is to dwell in divine love, to be filled with divine joy, and to be garrisoned in divine peace.

The outcome of this condition, in practical conduct towards others, will be "longsuffering, gentleness, goodness"; while the result of such conduct, in the building up of the character, will be "fidelity, meekness, temperance."

In the first three we have the inward disposition; in the second three, the external manifestation; and in the last three, the personal characteristic. This brings us to consider the fourth and last element in our progressive transformation into the image of God's Son.

Character. While the nature is something which is communicated instantaneously, character is that which can only be built up by degrees; it is something that is going on constantly.

As successive acts form habits, so habits combine to form character. "Character is consolidated habit." Every act of true obedience is a real contribution to the formation of Christian character. But we would stress true obedience. We often judge actions from what we see of them externally. But, as we know, there are two parts in all obedience—the outward act and the inward motive. The real value of the act is in its motive.

"Do you know what that silent work is which is going on in you? Oh builder, do you ever think of all the structures that are going up in these great cities? There are none that are building so fast and with so many hands as that structure of which you are the subject. . . . There are as many master workmen in you as there are separate faculties; and there are as many blows being struck as there are separate acts of emotion or volition. And this work is going on perpetually. Every single day these myriad forces are building, building, building. Here is a great structure going up point by point, story by story, although you are not conscious of it. *It is a building of character*. It is a building that is to stand. And the inspired Word warns you to take heed how you build it; to see to it that you have a foundation that shall endure; to make sure that you are building on it not for the hour in which you live but for that hour of revelation, that hour of testing, when that which hath been done shall be brought out and you shall be seen just as you are."

The Spirit of the Lord is upon Me, because He hath anointed Me to preach the gospel to the poor; He hath sent Me to heal the brokenhearted, to preach deliverance to the captives, and recovering of sight to the blind, to set at liberty them that are bruised, to preach the acceptable year of the Lord (Luke 4:18–19).

Where the Spirit of the Lord is, there is liberty (2 Corinthians 3:17).

Ye shall know the truth, and the truth shall make you free (John 8:32).

The perfect law of liberty (James 1:25).

Stand fast therefore in the liberty wherewith Christ hath made us free (Galatians 5:1).

My yoke is easy, and My burden is light (Matthew 11:30).

4

LIBERTY

FREEDOM is an essential characteristic of that life of fellowship with Christ into which the redeemed are called. The essence of being is life. The essence of *well*-being is freedom in life. There may, however, be life without liberty. The work of regeneration may have taken place, and hence the new nature may be there and heaven-born aspirations may be going forth from our quickened spirits, and yet our life may be anything but free.

Christ not only imparts life, He also provides that which is necessary for its emancipation—for its unfolding and growth.

Struggles may be true signs of vitality, but they are often the witness to a condition of bondage. Desperate efforts to set oneself free should be taken as evidence that we are no longer "dead in trespasses and sins"; but such conflicts must not be confounded with "the good fight of faith." Freedom is not the end but rather the condition of Christian conflict—of true victorious warfare. To fight so as to "withstand" and come off "more than conquerors," we must know what it is to "stand fast in the liberty wherewith Christ hath made us free" (Galatians 5:1).

Liberty consists in the unrestrained activities of life. "Only that existence can be called really free that lives and moves in full agreement with its proper being, that can unfold its powers unhindered and undisturbed" (Martensen). For this it is necessary that life—whether it be vegetable, animal, or spiritual—should be in its true and appropriate element. It is only there that it finds both its sustenance and its freedom. Thus the plant must have not only suitable soil, but air and moisture and sunshine. The surroundings do not originate the life, but they afford that which is essential for its expansion and development. In this unhindered activity its freedom consists.

And so in nature we say a creature is free when it can move in its own native element. The bird is free in the air, and the fish in the water. Take either of them out of its element and its liberty is gone. Change or modify the character of the element and you limit or destroy the freedom of the creature's life.

Through sin we have lost the inner principle of life, and we have forfeited also the sphere which is its true abode. Restoration consists in both the quickening of the spirit and its introduction into its appropriate environment. To be "born again" is to receive that quickening; and to be "in Christ" is to be in that environment. Spiritual liberty can be known, therefore, only by those who have life and are abiding in Him who is the true sphere of life. We cannot, then, take it for granted that every regenerate soul is of necessity in a state of spiritual liberty. Conversion is not all. Salvation means something far more than the possession of a divine, inner vital principle.

There is a threefold emancipation we may notice in connection with our experience of true freedom: liberty for the mind, the conscience, and the will.

Liberty for the mind. In harmony with the foregoing definitions of freedom, we may observe that man's intellect or understanding must have its proper environment. It must occupy its true sphere in order to be free. That sphere is the *truth*. As originally created, the mind of man was free because he dwelt in the truth. There was nothing in his moral or spiritual surroundings but what was in perfect agreement with his mental being. Since the Fall, however, everything is changed. His mind is in bondage, through darkness and ignorance and error. The apostle thus describes those who are in this state: "Having the understanding darkened, being alienated from the life of God through the ignorance that is in them because of the blindness of their heart" (Ephesians 4:18). Man fell through receiving Satan's lie. By this act he forfeited the truth; losing the truth, his mind lost its freedom.

Christ restores us to liberty by bringing us into the truth. "Ye shall know the truth, and the truth shall make you free" (John 8:32). Such is the freedom known and realized when we become spiritually enlightened. It is like the morning dawn—the light breaks into our inner being, and we become conscious that we have been brought into an illuminated atmosphere. We know and feel that our mental being has found its true element. What the air is to the bird, and what the water is to the fish, the truth of God is to our minds. As the bird spreads its wings, so our powers and faculties expand and find in this new element a liberty, an enlargement, that fills our souls with peculiar gladness.

But when we speak of the *truth* we must not understand by that term a mere abstraction. We must think of *Him* who declared, "I am—the truth." We must think of that living embodiment of truth "in whom we live and move and have our being." Saving faith means "believing *into*" Christ. It implies an actual transition from one sphere into another—from darkness to light. It is in Him who *is* the truth that we realize, therefore, our mental emancipation.

Liberty for the conscience. Bondage may arise from sin as well as from ignorance. Guilt on the conscience will rob the soul of all liberty. There can be no freedom of utterance, no holy boldness, no liberty in the presence of God if sin, in its guilt and defilement, lies on the conscience. "Having our hearts sprinkled from an evil conscience" (Hebrews 10:22) is essential in order to enter into the "holiest of all." An emancipated conscience is a purged conscience. When this is realized, the soul is in an atmosphere of peace. It is *in* that peace the conscience finds its freedom. But it is only through "the blood of His cross" that this can be known. When we see the meaning of Christ's death, when we accept it as that which brings us into a relation of reconciliation with God, we know what peace means. We see, then, not only that we stand on the work of peace but have been brought into Him who *is* our peace. The *conscience* finds its freedom in the atmosphere of divine *peace*.

Liberty for the will. It is the remark of a thoughtful

preacher, "that the weakness of human actions may be traced to the supremacy of passion—that the passions are too strong, and carry away the will with them, so that the will as a regulative force in man is crippled" (Canon Boyd Carpenter's *Hulsean Lectures*).

Man's will, by nature, is not free. It is the slave of fear or of desire. If the passions are evil, his will is the victim of a sinful tyranny. There may be light and knowledge without liberty. A man may see and know the right and yet shrink from doing it because of the fear of suffering or reproach. This is to be in a state of bondage. He may see the evil and know that it is his duty to avoid it, and yet he may be drawn to yield to it because of the pleasure that is more or less blended with it. How is liberty from such a condition to be brought about?

Suppose that the will is strengthened, and that by dint of a high sense of duty the man is enabled to rise superior to the power of his passions; shall we have in such a one an example of true liberty? Surely not.

As an able and vigorous writer observes: "We can make ourselves perform certain acts by an effort of the will, but this is a very different thing from making our inclinations go along with them" (Canon Mozley's *University Sermons*). What the will needs, in the first place, is not strengthening, but liberating. It must first be brought into its proper environment; there it finds its freedom. It may be weak, but it is no small matter that it is free—and being liberated, it is now prepared to be strengthened.

The element in which the will finds its freedom is the love of God.

The popular definition of liberty—namely, "to do as you like"—is, after all, not far from the truth. The glorified spirits are free and they do as they like; but being holy in their desires, they do what God likes. And so, just in proportion as man's affections are purified and he delights in the things that God delights in, he finds his freedom in doing as he likes. Whatever, therefore, purifies his desires also liberates his will. To set the will free, it follows it must be brought into the atmosphere of divine love. As the mind finds its liberty in Him who is the truth, and the conscience in Him who is our peace, so the will finds its freedom in Him who is the embodiment of perfect love.

"The criterion of the highest and perfect moral state of mind is pleasure—when good acts are not only done, but when we take pleasure in doing them. We are certainly bound to do them, whether we like it or not; and obedience for conscience sake, which is carried out against inclination, is deserving of all praise, and is constantly urged upon us in Scripture; but it is still an inferior moral state compared with that in which the inclinations themselves are on the side of good. For, looking into the real nature of the case, we cannot but call it a state of servitude when a man's affections do not go along with his work but he submits to duty as a yoke which a superior power or law imposes on him, even though that law be revealed to him through his own conscience" (Mozley, *University Sermons*).

We have, then, two stages of experience, both included in the life of the Christian—the one being animated chiefly by a sense of right, the other by the power of love. We may illustrate the two stages by two concentric circles—the outer circle representing the duty-life, and the inner circle the love-life. We may be within the first and yet not within the second; but it is impossible to be within the inner circle and not be within the outer circle also. So if we are "dwelling in love" we shall know what it is to do the right for its own sake as well as from inclination. It is not difficult to see which of the two conditions is the true life of liberty.

"The truth must be admitted, that many who belong visibly to the dispensation of the Spirit are still inwardly under the law in this sense, that their inclinations are not yet on the side of God's service, and that, if they perform their duty in any degree, it is only in obedience to a law, of the penalties of which they stand in just and proper fear, but not on the spiritual principles of love" (Mozley, *University Sermons*).

Hence, while faith makes all things possible, it is love that makes all things easy.

But if love is the secret of the highest kind of freedom, what love is it? Where are we to seek for it? Whence does it come? And how may we be brought to know it and live in it?

Shall we say, as some maintain, that there is "a root of love at the bottom of the human heart, which it has received from God, and which only requires the removal of the pressure of other things upon it to bring it out as the true part of man"? Surely not.

The love which casts out fear and sets us free is not human love, inherent in man, lying dormant within, and only waiting to be wakened and brought forth. "The air weighs heavily on such hollow bodies as are void of air; so God's law, and even God Himself, who reveals

Himself by means of the law, rests like a heavy, oppressive burden on souls who have not God within them" (Martensen). That sense of oppression gives the evidence that no kindred affection exists within them.

It is *divine love* that the soul needs. "The love of God" must be "shed abroad in our hearts" (Romans 5:5. Strictly *throughout*, not *into*, our hearts—*en* not *eis*, denoting the rich diffusion of God's love *within* our hearts; *en* also indicating the locality where the shedding abroad takes place).

"The love of God—this means, not our love to God, nor exactly the sense of God's love for us, but *God's love itself* for us" (Neil).

As Dr. Forbes observes: "The love here spoken of [Romans 5:5] is not God's love as merely *outwardly shown to us* but as *shed abroad in our hearts as a gift,* and is placed in connection with other Christian graces—patience and hope" (*Analytical Commentary on the Epistle to the Romans*).

This divine love "*becomes* our love to God" (Lange). The medium of this transfusion of the divine love in the heart is the Holy Spirit. He Himself first enters into the soul and then from within makes known to us God's love, and communicates it as a power molding our emotions, purposes and actions (Beet).

The expression "shed abroad" denotes plenitude of communication (Tholuck). As Philippi observes on the same text: "The love of God did not descend upon us as dew in drops, but as a stream which spreads itself through the whole soul, filling it with a consciousness of His presence and favor."

In the same connection we have another and still

more wonderful passage in the seventeenth of St. John's Gospel. At the close of our Lord's intercessory prayer we read: "And I have declared unto them Thy name, and will declare it: that the love wherewith Thou hast loved Me may be in them, and I in them" (John 17:26). Here again the love referred to is nothing short of God's own love. The truth declared is the indwelling of divine love. "When God's love *to* us comes to be *in* us, it is like the virtue which the loadstone gives the needle, inclining it to move towards the pole" (Lange). As Dr. Westcott remarks: "The possibility of such a consummation lies in the fact of the presence of the Son Himself in them." "The love of God in lighting on believers will not attach itself to aught that is defiled. For it will in truth light only on Jesus Himself, on Jesus living in them, and upon them as identified with Him and reflecting His holy image" (Godet).

In the same way that passage in St. John's Epistle is to be understood: "Behold, what manner of love the Father hath bestowed upon us" (1 John 3:1). "How many read these words as if the meaning were, Behold, what manner of love the Father hath *manifested* towards us. But here we have something more than a mere *demonstration* of love; the full power of divine love has *imparted itself to us as our own*, is a free *gift* to us; not only specific manifestations of the love of God, but *that love itself is given to us*" (Haupt). Or, as another puts it, "God has made His love our property" (Meyer). "God has not only *given* in love, but He has given love *itself*, made it our own, absolutely given it to us, so that *His love* is now *ours*" (Lange). Dr. Westcott remarks on this text, in his *Commentary on the Epistles of St. John:* "The love is not simply exhibited towards believers, but imparted to them. The divine love is, as it were, infused into them, so that it is their own, and becomes in them the source of a divine life (Romans 13:10). In virtue of this gift, therefore, they are inspired with a love which is like the love of God, and by this they truly claim the title of children of God, as partakers in His nature."

Then we have that marvelous statement in the fourth chapter of this same epistle (1 John 4:16, ASV), on which Dr. Westcott observes: "The nature of the believer must be conformed to the nature of God. . . . From the very nature of God, it follows as a necessary consequence that the life of self-devotion is a life in fellowship with Him. . . . 'He that abideth in love,' as the sphere in which his life is fulfilled, 'abideth in God, and God [abideth] in him.' He that so abides in love has risen to the heavenly order (Colossians 3:3) and found the power of divine fellowship for the accomplishment of earthly work."

One deeply taught in the spiritual life observes: "We must remember carefully to discriminate that it is not the way of our salvation that St. John is here speaking of. He assumes that those whom he is addressing are saved; for notice what comes immediately before is: 'Whosoever shall confess that Jesus is the Son of God'—that is salvation, that confession of faith is salvation—'God dwelleth in him, and he in God'—that is the union, consequent upon the faith, in the salvation, with the Son, and through the Son with the Father. . . . It is a very strong and eloquent term 'to *dwell* in love,' a *home* of love. And the promise of that home of love is more wonderful still—that God shall be our home. And then more stupendous beyond it—and we shall be God's home. He that has made his home in love has his home in God, and God has His home in him" (Rev. James Vaughan, Brighton).

It is in this home of divine love that the will is free. It is then that "God is the element of human volition" (Delitzsch). Finding our home is *God*, the bondage of external restraint is at an end. This is not a mere ideal. It is a possible experience! It is that "fullness of the blessing of Christ" which we may know even here in this life. Truth, peace, and love are no less realities than are the mind, the conscience, and the will.

It is by bringing each part of our being into its true environment that the Spirit accomplishes His work of emancipation. A life of mere duty is thus transformed into a life of liberty and delight. Let us suppose the case of one whose desires are only partially purified. Peace with God has been known and realized, but, owing to a want of liberty, this peace has become sadly marred. Incessant struggles and repeated failures have robbed the life of all joy. Such a one is told that conflict is one of the characteristics of the Christian life. He learns, moreover, from the Word of God that he is called to "fight the good fight of faith," and that being a soldier of the Cross he has to "put on the whole armour of God." Conflict, therefore, he sees clearly from Scripture, there must be.

But how often such a one concludes too hastily that the struggles he experiences constitute the Christian warfare! He does not distinguish between conflict and rebellion. The will may not be wholly yielded. It may be under the influence of some evil desire.

There can be no real peace or liberty for a soul in that condition. We can conceive of a case in which the will is strong and the passions are held well under control. And what have you? You have a life of outward abstinence from the evil and of conformity to the good, but not a life of joy and liberty. You have a man who walks conscientiously, it is true; but he knows nothing of real delight and freedom in the service of God.

The force of conscience and the power of will may be sufficient in many instances to keep the passions under restraint, so that in the main there is an absence of outward transgression, and, it may be, a good deal of zeal and activity in working for God. But, oh, what a sense of strain and perpetual bondage within! Christ's yoke is felt to be constantly pressing. It is not found to be easy, nor His burden to be light.

Now let us suppose such a one is brought under the power of a fuller and deeper work of the Holy Spirit. Let us suppose that divine love sanctifies his desires to the same degree that divine truth has emancipated his mind and divine peace his conscience. What then? A complete change takes place in his whole life. Because he begins to love the right and delights in acknowledging its excellence, he now finds it easy to do it. He begins to *like* what God commands; and it is never hard to do what one likes. Then he finds the truth, in his own experience, of those words, "His commandments are not grievous."

Here, then, lies the secret of liberty and delight in the service of the Lord.

Seek to grasp the glorious fact that you may have

Christ as divine love filling your soul. Just as the alabaster box was in the house and its presence may not have been known, so Christ has been a long time with many of His disciples and they have not known Him; that is, they have been comparatively ignorant of His glorious fullness. But no sooner was the box broken, and the ointment shed abroad, than the odor filled the house. So when the love of God is poured forth by the Holy Ghost—when the infinite treasures of divine love stored up in Christ are disclosed, revealed *in* us, shed abroad in our hearts by the Holy Ghost—their subduing, liberating, and transforming influences begin at once to be seen and felt. Their cleansing and purifying effects on our thoughts and desires are realized. We begin to learn then what our blessed Lord meant when He said, "Blessed are the pure in heart, for they shall see God" (Matthew 5:8).

But do you ask, How am I to get this love? "Love," one has said, "cannot be produced by a direct action of the soul upon itself. A man in a boat cannot move it by pressing it from within."

It is not by straining and struggling that this blessed condition is brought about; it comes by a very real dedication of ourselves to God for this very purpose, and with this as the special end and aim in view. Just lie quietly before Him. Open all the avenues of your being, and let Him come in and take possession of every chamber. Especially give Him your heart—the very seat of your desires, the throne of your affections. Yield all up to Him, and the Lord will enter, bringing with Him all the riches of His grace and glory, turning your life of duty into a life of liberty and love.

But we all, with open face beholding as in a glass the glory of the Lord, are changed [being changed] into the same image from glory to glory, even as by the Spirit of the Lord (2 Corinthians 3:18).

Both He that sanctifieth and they who are sanctified [being sanctified] are all of one (Hebrews 2:11).

For by one offering He hath perfected for ever them that are [being] sanctified (Hebrews 10:14).

I am the LORD your God: ye shall therefore sanctify yourselves, and ye shall be holy; for I am holy (Leviticus 11:44).

Let us cleanse ourselves from all filthiness of the flesh and spirit, perfecting holiness in the fear of God (2 Corinthians 7:1).

Yield yourselves unto God (Romans 6:13).

Present your bodies a living sacrifice (Romans 12:1).

Jesus, who of God is made unto us . . . sanctification (1 Corinthians 1:30).

For their sakes I sanctify Myself, that they also might be sanctified through the truth (John 17:19).

5

SANCTIFICATION

IN ORDER to avoid the confusion that often exists, even in the minds of intelligent believers, on this important subject, it is necessary that we should distinguish between the different senses in which sanctification is contemplated in the Scriptures. One reason for the perplexity, we venture to think, is found in the fact that different aspects of the same truth are often confused. We should clearly recognize the distinction, for instance, between three things: sanctification as a process, as an act or attitude of consecration, and as a gift. Let us consider that first which is the best understood, and not because it is the first in the order of time.

1. Sanctification may be considered as a PROCESS; that is, as a work wrought in the soul of the believer by the Holy Spirit, subsequently to regeneration. Of both regeneration and renewal the Holy Spirit is the Author, but the two things are not the same. Regeneration is an instantaneous communication of divine life to the soul. It is not capable of degrees; no believer is more or less regenerate than another. "But this work of sanctification is *progressive*, and admits of degrees. One may be

more sanctified and more holy than another, even
though he is truly sanctified and truly holy. It is begun
at once, and carried on gradually" (Owen on the work
of the Holy Spirit).

We do not intend, however, to inquire how the Holy
Spirit carries on His work, our present purpose being to
ascertain from Scripture what are the chief features of
that work.

We learn, for instance, that it is gradual and progressive, from such passages as 2 Corinthians 3:18. Our
spiritual transformation is there described as still going
on. "We are changed [or being changed] into the same
image from glory to glory, even as by the Spirit of the
Lord." The change here described is that gradual conformity to Christ which takes place during this present
life. This is something more than a mere reformation of
character, and is brought about by something higher
than mere moral culture or discipline; it is transfiguration. The word occurs altogether in four places (Matthew 17:2; Mark 9:2; Romans 12:2; 2 Corinthians 3:18).
The nature of the change is exemplified in what took
place at our Lord's transfiguration. "It would appear
that the light shone not upon Him from without, but out
of Him from within." He was all irradiated with celes-
tial glory. So the change that takes place in the gradual
sanctification of the believer is by virtue of a divine
power that works from within. "Instead of the mind of a
man being developed by the form and fashion of his
age, he receives within himself the source of a new
life. . . . From within and not from without, from the
mind and not from the world, by the birth of what is
new and not by the growth of what is old, the whole

aspect of human nature is transformed" (Wace)—just as the bud is transformed into the flower, the blossom into the fruit, the acorn into the oak, by a vital power that works from within. This power is not in man by nature; it is not a force that has been pent up, needing only to be liberated in order to produce the transformation. It is God the Holy Ghost who is the Author of the change; it is the divine indwelling Spirit alone who restores fallen man to the image of God, making him a partaker of the divine nature (2 Peter 1:4).

Sanctification considered from this point of view is thus seen to be a *process*. Such also is the nature of all spiritual progress and growth—a progressive and gradual development of the new creation within the believer.

Now it is evident that in that sense our sanctification can never in this life reach a point beyond which there is to be no further progress. It can never, therefore, be said to be complete. So long as there is room for a fuller manifestation of the divine image, the work cannot be said to be completed.

2. But sanctification may be looked at from another point of view—as an ATTITUDE. It may be regarded in relation to our own individual condition and conduct—as personal separation from all known sin on the one hand, and dedication to God on the other. The root-thought of sanctity is separateness. A man sanctifies himself when he separates himself from that which is evil and impure. "I am the LORD your God: ye shall therefore sanctify yourselves, and ye shall be holy; for I am holy" (Leviticus 11:44). So again in the New Testament we have the exhortation addressed to those who

were already set apart unto God: "Let us cleanse ourselves from all filthiness of the flesh and spirit, perfecting holiness in the fear of God" (2 Corinthians 7:1).

In this aspect sanctification may be regarded as a personal and definite act of consecration to God. Following the initial act, the habit or attitude of surrender is formed; and as progress is made, so the thoroughness of dedication to God deepens and increases.

We may take the word "yield" as expressive of the main idea involved in such a personal consecration; it puts before us what we may call the human side of the doctrine of holiness.

In the twelfth chapter of the Epistle to the Romans the apostle beseeches those who were already Christians "to present their bodies a living sacrifice." What did the apostle mean? To "present" is to "yield." The same word occurs in chapter 6, verses 13, 16 and 19. Now what is it to yield? It is to cease to resist. That there may be a resistance to the will of God even in those who have been quickened by the Spirit, no believer who knows any thing of his own heart can deny. This resistance is one of the main hindrances to the exercise of faith. It was so with Jacob at Peniel. "And there wrestled a man with him until the breaking of the day." Who was this that confronted Jacob, and whom Jacob resisted? It was none other than the Angel of the Covenant; it was the LORD Himself who laid His hand on Jacob.

Though God had not forsaken Jacob, Jacob had been following in the main his own will during his sojourn in Padan-aram. Twenty years before he had been favored with a wonderful vision, in which God had revealed to him the way of access in prayer and the way of blessing from God to man; he had seen God in covenant with His people. If Jacob apprehended there at Bethel nothing more, he beheld at least God as his Protector and Provider and Guide. And this vision drew from him a vow: "If God will be with me, and will keep me in this way that I go, and will give me bread to eat, and raiment to put on, so that I come again to my father's house in peace, then shall the LORD be my God" (Genesis 28:20–21). But how had it been with him during those twenty years? He had sojourned with Laban, and there he had pursued the same course that he had previously followed with his brother and his father—a course of meanness and deception. God had sent him trials and had during those years been contending with him, bringing back to his memory and his conscience the evil of his own ways; but Jacob was still the same Jacob—the supplanter—not humbled, not broken, full of carnal policy and self-seeking.

But now comes the crisis. Jacob's will must be broken. In this conflict, Jacob's *wrestling* must not be confounded with Jacob's *clinging*. So long as he wrestled—that is, resisted—the conflict lasted. But at last the resistance ceased.

"And when He [the LORD] saw that He prevailed not against him, He touched the hollow of his thigh; and the hollow of Jacob's thigh was out of joint, as He wrestled with him" (Genesis 32:25). All power to resist was now at an end.

This passage in Jacob's history has a parallel in the life of many a child of God. How many can trace a similar crisis in God's dealing with them!

The power of resistance—which is self-will—being broken, the strength to cling—which is faith—is now brought into exercise. So we see Jacob, the moment his thigh was out of joint, no longer wrestling but clinging—no longer as an antagonist resisting an enemy, but as a suppliant in an attitude of earnest entreaty: "I will not let Thee go, except Thou bless me."

This was the power by which Jacob prevailed; and it is to this act of clinging, as the symbol of faith, that the prophet Hosea refers: "By his strength he had power with God: yea, he had power over the angel, and prevailed: he wept and made supplication unto him" (Hosea 12:3–4).

Thus we learn that if we would cling with a victorious faith we must first yield in a spirit of entire submission. You cannot cling until you have ceased to resist.

But yielding means also ceasing to withhold. "My son, give Me thine heart." In other words, let God have full possession, not only of the spirit and the soul, but of all your physical powers. Yield every member up to Him. If we regard "the essential condition of man as subsisting in three concentric circles, the innermost being his spirit, the inner his soul, and the external his body" (Delitzsch), we can see how the progress in his practical consecration to God takes place. To yield is to withhold nothing. The spirit being quickened presents the body as well as the soul to the Lord. "I beseech you therefore, brethren, . . . present your *bodies*." Every power of mind or body is dedicated to His service and committed into His keeping.

"This verse [Romans 12:1] looks upon the man within as the priest who lays upon the altar not the body

of a dead sheep, but his own living body. . . . Our
body has now the sacredness associated in the mind of
a Jew with the animals laid on the brazen altar; . . .
and presentation to God makes our body *holy*, as it did
the sacrificial animals (Exodus 29:37). Henceforth they
exist only to work out God's purposes" (Beet).

And again, yielding also means ceasing to struggle.
No longer trying to keep oneself up—putting forth vigorous efforts to keep oneself from sinking—but casting
all upon Him who is able to keep us from falling.

But this yielding, it may be objected, surely is not an
act done once for all. However definite and real that act
may have been, does it not need continually to be repeated? We would answer that if we suppose a relapse
to have taken place—if, having presented ourselves, we
have afterwards withdrawn the gift—then of course
repetition is necessary. But this surely is not the life to
which we are called. Having yielded ourselves, spirit,
soul, and body to Him, what we now have to do is daily
to recognize and confirm that act, and in this way the
act once definitely accomplished becomes an attitude
constantly maintained.

It is interesting to note what one able commentator
(Dr. David Brown) remarks about this act of consecration: "A significant transition has been noticed here [in
Romans 6:13] from one tense to another. In the first
clause, 'Neither yield ye your members instruments of
unrighteousness,' the *present* tense is used (*pari-
stanete*), denoting the *habitual* practice of men in their
old, unregenerate state; in the next clause, 'but yield
yourselves unto God,' it is the aorist (*paristesate*) sug-
gesting the *one act for all*, of self-surrender, which the

renewed believer performs immediately on his passing from death to life, and to which he only gets his continuous seal in all his after life" (*Critical and Experimental Commentary.* See Appendix, Note D).

To this important note, however, we would merely add this question: If the apostle had felt sure that these Christians at Rome had *immediately on their conversion* thus surrendered themselves to God, would he have deemed it necessary *now* to press upon them so earnestly this definite act of consecration? The truth is, the apostle does not assume or take for granted that all those Christian converts were really walking in a condition of practical consecration to God.

Looking at this aspect of our subject, then, we may note two things of paramount importance. The first is the condition of the will; the second is the attitude of our faith. To be wholly the Lord's—to let go one's will so that henceforth Christ is to lead me and plan for me, and have His way with me in everything—is to be ready to be separated from many ways and things to which naturally we cling very tenaciously. It is to let Him have the whole heart, to reign there supreme. The will is not really yielded if we have any reserves. We have not let go our moorings if there is still but one rope that keeps our little boat to the shore. We may have "slipped" many a cable that has kept us to the land, but if one single rope remains we are still held fast. We are not yet wholly the Lord's in the sense of practical consecration.

But suppose this has been done, and that so far as the light has enabled you to see, everything has been laid on the altar. Then comes the question of faith.

What is your attitude to your faith? As to justification, you are no longer seeking but resting; you are no longer anxiously praying about that, but you can thankfully praise Him. That need then has been met.

And can He not meet your need as to sanctification? Your present and continuous need in this respect can only be met by a present and continuous provision. That provision is in Christ. He who commands us to ask commands us also to receive. To be in an attitude of trust is to be receptive, and being receptive we find that we lack nothing; for Christ is our sanctification. But this is the aspect in which we have next to consider the subject.

3. Lastly, sanctification in its fullest sense is a GIFT.

Nothing is more essential in order to dwell in God's presence than holiness. Forgiveness of sins is not all we need. Peace alone is not sufficient. Nor is a perfect righteousness which places us in a position of acceptance with God all that is provided for us in the gospel. There must be likeness to God . . . conformity of heart . . . oneness of nature.

But what God requires He first provides. This is one of the chief features of grace: "all things are of God." And grace characterizes each step in the believer's progress. Salvation from sin is possible only because we are not left to ourselves—to our merits, our own efforts, or our own resources. He is the "God of all grace." The moment we act as if we had to meet His demands *from ourselves*, that moment we forsake the ground of *grace*.

Salvation is of grace because it is a gift. It is all included in Christ.

Now we know that without holiness no man shall see the Lord (Hebrews 12:14); and yet we believe that Christ is able to save the sinner even at the very last moment of his earthly existence. Taking holiness only in the one sense of a process or work wrought in us by the Holy Ghost suggests a difficulty. It may reasonably be asked, If without holiness no man can see the Lord, what becomes of those who, like the penitent thief, come to Christ at the eleventh hour? They have no time or opportunity for the growth and development of sanctification.

But the difficulty leads one to inquire, What does the Scripture mean by holiness? That it often refers to the process which is wrought in us by the Holy Spirit all must admit, but that Christ Himself is made of God unto us sanctification as well as righteousness, many of God's children fail to understand. One of God's greatest gifts—bound up in His "unspeakable Gift"—is that of holiness.

But what is holiness? How does God teach us what holiness means? Does He give us an abstract definition—a mere verbal description? No, He sends us His Son. He sets before us a Person, a living embodiment, His own ideal of holiness.

Jesus is God's conception of a perfect man. In His life on earth we have set before us God's ideal of divine holiness manifested and unfolded in a real human nature.

God sent His Son not only to be the "Just One," who should fulfill all righteousness and meet all the claims of His righteous law, He sent Him to be the "Holy One," who should satisfy all the desires of a Father's heart—as the One in whom He could ever delight. He was therefore made wisdom to us from God, even righteousness and sanctification.

But how did Christ become sanctification unto us? He Himself declares, "For their sakes I sanctify Myself, that they also might be sanctified through the truth" (John 17:19); or, to make sanctification possible, He sanctifies Himself. Christ here puts before us the *progressive* aspect of His own sanctification. Already He was sanctified by the Father. "Say ye of Him, whom the Father hath sanctified," etc. (John 10:36). But He speaks now of His own personal consecration to the will of His Father, which should secure the sanctification of His believing ones.

What He would subsequently unfold and develop in those who should be brought into living union with Himself He first realizes in Himself. Their holiness should be essentially the same as that which was being accomplished in His own person.

It is important here to bear in mind that "to *sanctify* is not synonymous with to *purify*. To purify oneself implies that one is defiled; to sanctify oneself is simply to consecrate to God the natural powers of the soul and of the body, as soon as they come into exercise" (Godet).

He who was from the beginning absolutely holy *became* our holiness. He who was from the first absolutely perfect *became* perfected. Christ became in Himself, through trial and suffering, what He would afterwards be in us; namely, sanctification. The holiness of His believing ones should be the result and outcome of His own indwelling.

And so we read, "He *learned obedience* by the things which He suffered" (Hebrews 5:8). This denotes not a transition from disobedience to obedience, but the development in His own person and experience of the principle of entire consecration to God in connection with the trials and sufferings of a real human life, which has constituted Him the Captain of our salvation. "Being *perfected* He *became* the author of eternal salvation" (Hebrews 5:9). The "perfecting" of Jesus as the "Leader of salvation" was historically accomplished in His person, and in this manner: by His having actually passed through and completed His career of human trial and suffering (See Appendix, Note E).

He traversed the whole realm of faith; He ascended the whole scale, from the lowest to the highest step; He has gone through the whole course. He is the Leader and the Perfecter of faith (Hebrews 12:2); He has preceded the whole company of believers. He is the princely Leader of the faith-life; He came to fulfill the true ideal of faith. He not only taught it in precept, illustrated it in parable and encouraged it by miracle, He exemplified it in His own life.

He became one in whom faith was exhibited in perfection. Faith cannot be exhibited without trial. Trial must have its course. "Knowing this, that the trying of your faith worketh patience. But let patience have her perfect work, that ye may be perfect and entire, wanting nothing" (James 1:3–4).

Christ then, who is the Pattern and Example, has also become the "Author of eternal salvation," not merely as the external source but as the indwelling Life—the vital *Cause* of our personal transformation. And this He becomes to all "those *obeying* Him." Having reached the goal Himself, He becomes the cause or origin of their sanctification.

From this we learn that to become holy we must possess the "Holy One." It must be Christ in us. Without *that* holiness "no man shall see the Lord." Holiness of walk flows from the Holy One. Conformity to the will of God in conduct is the outcome of conformity to the will of God in heart and mind, and this can only be brought about by enshrining Christ as Lord in our hearts (1 Peter 3:15). That is, "Render to Christ in the inmost chamber of your being the reverence which belongs to Him who claims to be your Proprietor and Master" (Beet). Possess the source and you have the stream. This is that "holiness without which no man shall see the Lord."

But although this Gift is a present possession in the case of every believer, how many there are that fail to apprehend what it is they really do possess in Christ! It is one thing to be the owner of an estate; it is another thing to know what it contains. It is one thing to be in actual possession of the property, another thing to know the vast treasures of wealth that lie beneath the surface. So we may have received Christ Jesus the Lord into our hearts and yet may still have seen but little comparatively of the riches of grace and of glory stored up in Him for our daily realization.

And therefore, though Christ is ours—we have Him as a present possession—we must still follow on to know Him more perfectly. He must be ever the object of our daily aspirations. "Follow . . . that holiness, without which no man shall see the Lord." This implies activity, earnestness, diligence, zeal. To follow after an object is to have it constantly before you; you do not lose sight of it. It dwells in your thoughts; it becomes a part of your very life; it enters into your practice; it stamps your character. That which is the object of your desire and the aim of your energies will have a transforming influence on your life.

But this is a very different thing from saying that our likeness to Christ is just the result of a mere imitation of Jesus Christ. Christ is our sanctification in a far higher sense than that in which He is our pattern. He is our holiness because He Himself dwells in us, to control our whole moral being, to transfigure our whole lives, and to become in us the spring of all our thoughts and words and deeds.

But lest, by dwelling on the human side of Christ's earthly course as exhibiting God's ideal of holiness, we should for a moment lose sight of His essential deity, and hence the necessity of that deity in connection with our sanctification, we would here add some valuable remarks by the gifted author whose writings we have already frequently quoted, Professor Godet:

"All that you withdraw from the essential and personal divinity of Christ you take away from the reality of that holiness which constitutes your glorious destiny. I am struck by two expressions in this passage [Galatians 2:20] and by their instructive connection: 'The Son of God, who loved me,' and 'Christ liveth in me.' A man could not live in another man. A man can leave us his memory, his example, his teaching; but he cannot live again in us. If Jesus is only a holy man, complete and normal Christian sanctification is necessarily reduced to the sincere effort to follow and emulate him; and the Church would be nothing more than an association of well-disposed people, united together for the purpose of doing good, while studying their pattern, Jesus Christ. This is the level to which the most elevated and the most glorious idea of the gospel will immediately descend when once the crown of deity has been snatched from the head of Christ.

"But, as Scripture and experience both teach us, true Christian holiness is something more than effort, an aspiration of man: it is a communication of God to man; it is Christ in person who comes and dwells in us by the Holy Spirit. Thus St. Paul calls Christ not only our righteousness, but also our sanctification. And in St. John's Gospel Jesus expresses Himself thus: 'I will not leave you comfortless: I will come to you'; 'at that day'—the day of the coming of the Holy Ghost—'ye shall know that I am in My Father, and ye in Me, and I in you'; 'He that loveth Me shall be loved by My Father, and . . . We will come unto him, and make Our abode with him'; 'because I live, ye shall live also.' Who must He be, He who not only comes and dwells in us by the Holy Spirit, but whose indwelling is, at the same time, the indwelling of the Father? 'Without'—or, out of—'Me ye can do nothing,' continues Jesus; 'I am the Vine, ye are the branches; he that abideth in Me and I in him, the same bringeth forth much fruit.' The Spirit 'shall glorify Me.'

"The divine Spirit can never be said to communicate a man to other men. The divine Spirit does not glorify a man in the heart and in the life of other men. The divine Spirit glorifies a divine Being, the Son, who in His turn glorifies the Father. This truth is expressed in the form also of baptism, and is at the same time the secret of Christian sanctification; for *holiness is Christ*, and God in Christ dwelling in us by the Holy Spirit. And the Church? The Church is not only a voluntary association of sincere imitators of Jesus Christ, it is the *body of Christ*, the living organ which He fills with His plenitude" (Godet).

And so in His Church Christ is still on earth fulfilling that glorious declaration, "Lo, I am with you alway, even unto the end of the world." And this apprehension of Christ as our sanctification does not in the least detract from the honor due to the Holy Ghost as our sanctifier. Both facts are not only in the most perfect harmony, but are necessary the one to the other.

"Perhaps it will be asked," writes Professor Godet, "what is the connection between the passages in which our sanctification is attributed to the Holy Spirit and those in which it is attributed to Christ Himself living in us? (Galatians 2:20).

"The answer is easy. In reality these two classes of expression refer to one and the same fact. What is the work of the Holy Spirit? It is to impart Christ to us, with everything that is His, and to make Him live again in us—as the grain of wheat which lies dead in the earth is made by the power of nature to live again in each of the grains in the ear. And, on the other hand, by what means does Christ live in us? By the operation of the Holy Spirit. There takes place in believers, by the power of that divine Agent, an effect similar to that which produced the miraculous birth of Jesus Christ. 'My little children,' said St. Paul, 'of whom I travail in birth again until Christ is formed in you'" (Galatians 4:19).

Herein is My Father glorified, that ye bear much fruit (John 15:8).

Being fruitful in every good work (Colossians 1:10).

From Me is thy fruit found (Hosea 14:8).

Always bearing about in the body the dying of the Lord Jesus, that the life also of Jesus might be made manifest in our body (2 Corinthians 4:10).

That I may know Him, and the power of His resurrection, and the fellowship of His sufferings, being made conformable unto His death (Philippians 3:10).

I am crucified with Christ: nevertheless I live; yet not I, but Christ liveth in me (Galatians 2:20).

If we walk in the light, as He is in the light, we have fellowship one with another, and the blood of Jesus Christ His Son cleanseth us from all sin (1 John 1:7).

6

CONFORMITY TO
THE DEATH OF CHRIST

PRACTICAL holiness is put before us in the Scriptures under the figure of *fruit*. But what is fruit? It is the deposit of the sap. It is the final result of all the inner activities of the tree—the outcome of the hidden life, which, beginning with the root, passes through the stem into the branch, and finally manifests itself in bud, blossom, and fruit. When the fruit is formed and ripened, the great purpose of the tree's activity and growth is reached; the life has completed its cycle.

Fruit, therefore, illustrates that side of the spiritual life that is sacrificed for the good of others. Fruit is "the produce of the branch by which men are refreshed and nourished. The fruit is not for the branch but for those who come to carry it away. As soon as the fruit is ripe the branch gives it off—to commence afresh its work of beneficence, preparing its fruit for yet another season. A fruit-bearing tree lives not for itself, but wholly for those to whom its fruit brings refreshment and life. And so the branch exists only and entirely for the sake of the fruit. To make glad the husbandman is its object, its safety, and its glory" (Rev. Andrew Murray). "Herein is My Father glorified, that ye bear much fruit" (John 15:8).

Practical holiness, therefore, is not something that has to be manufactured. Something more than even a perfect pattern is needed in order for one to be conformed to the image of God's Son, for holiness is no mere question of imitation.

"Christ's life unfolded itself from a divine germ, planted centrally in His nature, which grew as naturally as a flower from a bud. This flower may be imitated; but one can always tell an artificial flower. The human form may be copied in wax, yet somehow one never fails to detect the difference. And this precisely is the difference between a native growth of Christian principle and the moral copy of it. The one is natural, the other mechanical; the one is a growth, the other an accretion. Now this, according to modern biology, is the fundamental distinction between the living and the not living, between an organism and a crystal. The living organism grows, the dead crystal increases. The first grows vitally from within, the last adds new particles from the outside. The whole difference between the Christian and the moralist lies here. The Christian works from the center, the moralist from the circumference. The one is an organism, in the center of which is planted by the living God a living germ. The other is a crystal, very beautiful it may be, but, only a crystal; it lacks the vital principle of growth" (Prof. Drummond).

So it is possible to perform duties and do good works and call them fruit. "If you were to tie half a dozen bunches of grapes on your old umbrella, that would not make a vine. You may tie them on very carefully, but they will not grow. But that is just what multitudes of people are trying to do" (Canon Wilberforce).

Practical holiness is not something that begins by *doing* but by *being*. It is not something to be built up, as you build a house, by adding brick to brick. It is not "a mosaic of moralities, nor a compilation of merits, nor a succession of acts. It is a growth" (Bishop Huntingdon).

There may be a good deal of outward activity in work that is really good, and yet no "fruit." What the apostle desired on behalf of the Colossian converts was that they might be "*fruitful* in every good work" (Colossians 1:10); in other words, that their service should be the direct outcome of a divine, indwelling, vital principle. It is possible to be zealous and active and busy in good works, and yet to continue unfruitful. Where there is real fruit the current of activity will flow from the center to the circumference.

What then is the Source of all practical holiness? It must have a source. Every river has a spring. In vital union with all fruit there must be a root. What then is the source of our fruitfulness? Not our renewed nature. "That which is born of the Spirit is spirit" (John 3:6); through the operation of God the Holy Spirit a spiritual nature has been imparted. But "fruit" is not the outcome of our new nature any more than in the vine fruit is the produce of the branch. The branch bears it, but the root produces it. It is the "fruit of the Spirit"—the Holy Spirit. A bad tree cannot yield good fruit. Regeneration is essential in order that the fruit should be good. But the new nature is not the source. It is Christ Himself. There is only *one source* of all holy living;

there is only *one holy life*. "From Me is thy fruit found" (Hosea 14:8). "I am the life," not simply because I am the pattern of a perfect life, or because I am the bestower of the gift of life, nor yet because I am the vital principle itself. Christ is the Spring itself. "With Thee is the fountain of life" (Psalm 36:9).

It is Christ living within us. "Not I," says the apostle, though I am redeemed. "Not I," though I am regenerate, and have eternal life. "I live; yet not I, but Christ liveth in me" (Galatians 2:20).

It was this that Christ promised in the fourth chapter of St. John's Gospel. "The water that I shall give him shall become *in him a well* of water springing up into everlasting life" (John 4:14). There is no progress in our appropriation of Christ as the life; there is, however, a progress in our *heart-knowledge* of that fact. We see first the life in its source (John 1:4), then in its bestowal (John 3:16), then in its indwelling (John 4:14), and then in its practical outflow (John 7:38). It is in this last stage that we have the "fruit," the outcome of an indwelling Christ.

Here, then, is the source of all practical holiness. It is important to lay the emphasis on that word "*liveth*." "Christ LIVETH in me."

What then is needed in order that this indwelling life should bring forth fruit abundantly unto God?

It is clear that divine life can need nothing from man to increase its vitality. It does not need our efforts to make it live. Think what it is we really possess, if Christ is in us. It was no mere figure of speech that the apostle employed when he declared that Christ was living in him. And what was true of him may be equally true of us. What then is it we possess? We have *Him* in whom all fullness of life actually dwells, in whom infinite resources are stored up for our use. Everything needed for continual growth, for perpetual freshness, and for abundant fruitfulness are found in Him. All power, all purity, and all fullness—absolutely everything needed to make all grace abound towards us, in us, and through us—are stored up in Him who truly dwells within us.

Since this is so, what then is needed? Shall we try to help Christ to live in us? Shall we try to make Christ more living? Shall we help Him to put forth His own power in us? Shall we try, in other words, to grow—to produce fruit? Surely not. And yet is not this the grand mistake multitudes are making? Something, however, has to be done. Something *is* needed to deepen our spiritual life. All Christians have Christ, and possess therefore all the resources of spiritual power and abundant fruitfulness; and yet not all Christians are abounding in fruit unto God. What is the reason for this?

It is here: though we cannot make Christ more living, though we cannot add to His infinite fullness of life and purity and power, we may be hindering the manifestation of that life.

One of the most serious hindrances is unbelief. This lies at the root of every other hindrance. But it may be urged that Christ has power to overcome this hindrance, that He is able to break through this obstacle. And we know, of course, that He is able, that He could sweep away the barrier of all human unbelief. But is this the method of His working? Is it the law of His dealing with men?

We see Jesus entering His home village. There were multitudes of poor and needy ones there. And He was ready to bless them. Surely the sick and maimed would be brought in crowds to His feet! But what do we read? "And He did not many mighty works there *because of their unbelief*" (Matthew 13:58). Not that there was no manifestation of His power. "He laid His hands upon a few sick folk, and healed them." But "He could there do *no mighty* work" (Mark 6:5). His power was omnipotent, but it conditioned itself, as infinite power always does in the world; and by this limitation it was not lessened but was glorified as moral and spiritual power.

But the incident throws light on many a passage in our own spiritual experience. The weakness and failure we have known arose not from an absence of power in Him who has made us His dwelling place, but from the lack of trust and confidence in Him which He is ever demanding of us.

We have limited the Holy One by our unbelief. We have "set a mark" on the extent of His power to overcome and deliver, to keep and to save.

What then is needed for the deepening of our spiritual life is the removal of every hindrance; and when we begin with unbelief, we lay the axe at the root of every other hindrance.

But it is just here that the difficulty lies. It may be answered: "By showing that it is a question of faith and not of effort, you do not remove the difficulty, you only shift it to another platform. How can I make myself more believing? I know it is because of my unbelief that I fail; but how am I to get more faith?"

This brings us to the main point of this chapter. The truth is, we need two powers: a power to remove the hindrances, and a power to produce the fruit; a power to separate from us the evil, and a power to transform into us the good.

This twofold power is found in Christ. There is the power of His death and the power of His life. We do not bid goodbye to the first because we have been brought to live in the second. Nay, the condition of knowing the power of His resurrection lies in "being made comformable unto His death" (Philippians 3:10).

The true life, that which triumphs over sin and "does not cease from yielding fruit," is a life that springs up *out of death.*

There is a deep spiritual meaning in those words of the apostle, which we fail to grasp at first sight, "Always bearing about in the body the dying"—or the putting to death (*nekrosin*)—"of the Lord Jesus, that the life also of Jesus might be made manifest in our body" (2 Corinthians 4:10).

Death is here put before us as the condition of life. The continual manifestation of the life depends upon the constant conformity to the death.

Death means separation, and life means union. By being brought more and more into sympathy with Christ's death unto sin we become more and more thoroughly separated from its service and defilement. It is not merely separation from sinning, it is a separation from the old self-life. The great hindrance to the manifestation of the Christ-life is the presence and activity of the self-life. This needs to be terminated and set aside. Nothing but "the putting to death of the Lord

Jesus Christ" can accomplish this. Conformity to His death means a separation in heart and mind from the old source of activity and the motives and aims of the old life.

This "conformity" is the condition for the manifestation of the divine life. As we have already observed, "the life of Jesus" does not need our energy or our efforts to make it more living. All that God requires is that we should fall in with those conditions which are essential for the removal of the hindrances. Let those conditions be complied with, and at once the life springs forth spontaneously and without strain or effort. Though we can neither originate nor strengthen it by direct efforts of our own, we may indirectly increase its manifestations by complying with the divinely appointed conditions.

Our part consists in getting down into the death of Christ; His part is to live out His own life in us, just as the waters spring forth from the fountain. Then we shall know what the apostle meant when he said, "Christ *liveth* in me." Where Christ thus dwells in unhindered activity, there will be steady growth, perpetual freshness, and abundant fruitfulness; and the life will be marked by ease and spontaneity, because it will be natural.

From this we see that it is impossible to exaggerate the importance of understanding the meaning of His death. We must see that He not only died "for sin" but "unto sin." In the first of these senses He died alone; we could not die with Him. He trod the winepress alone; as the sin offering, He alone became the propitiation for our sins. But in the second, we died *with* Him. We must know what it is to be brought into sympathy with Him in His death unto sin. Oneness with Christ in that sense is the means of becoming practically separated not only from sinful desires but also from the old self-life. And this assimilation to the dying Christ is not an isolated act but a condition of mind ever to be maintained, and to go on deepening. "Arm yourselves with the same mind: for he that hath suffered in the flesh hath ceased from sin" (1 Peter 4:1).

Identification with the death of Christ is the great truth we learn in the Lord's Supper. In the broken bread and the poured-out wine, what have we but the symbols of His death? What is it that we especially dwell upon and make prominent in that sacrament? "Ye do show forth His *death* till He come." And by partaking of those elements we become identified with Him in that death. We become practically partakers of His life in proportion as we enter into His death, as we are made conformable in heart and mind to His death.

Wherever the blood of Christ is referred to in the Scripture, it means invariably His blood *shed*. The "blood," we learn from the Old Testament (Leviticus 17:10–11), is the life. "For the life of the flesh is in the blood." In consequence of possessing this character it could not be eaten; it was to be reserved "to make an atonement for your souls upon the altar." The clause, "for it is the blood that maketh an atonement for the soul," may be more correctly rendered, "for the blood maketh atonement by means of the soul"; *i.e.,* by means of the life which the blood contains. The blood is the vehicle of the animal's life; it represents that life. When it is shed—poured out—it represents that life as sacrificed: in other words, the *death* of the animal. The shed blood stands for the death of the victim.

Now when we speak of "the blood of Christ," we mean the life poured out, sacrificed; *i.e.*, His *death*.

There is a power in His death to separate us from sin. All cleansing is separating; when a garment is cleansed, it is separated from that which defiled it.

So "the blood of Christ cleanseth"—*i.e.*, the death of Christ separates—"from every sin." The more thoroughly we are brought into oneness with that death, the more fully shall we know what it is to be "cleansed from all unrighteousness."

In the consecration of Aaron and his sons we see these great principles shadowed forth with wonderful clearness.

God commanded Moses: "Then shalt thou kill the ram, and take of his blood, and put it upon the tip of the right ear of Aaron, and upon the tip of the right ear of his sons, and upon the thumb of their right hand, and upon the great toe of their right foot, and sprinkle the blood upon the altar round about. And thou shalt take of the blood that is upon the altar, and of the anointing oil, and sprinkle it upon Aaron, and upon his garments, and upon his sons, and upon the garments of his sons with him: and he shall be hallowed, and his garments, and his sons, and his sons' garments with him" (Exodus 29:20–21).

We see here in type that which may be true in the experience of God's children. The ear, the hand, and the foot are all to be consecrated to God. Conformity to the death of Christ—contact with the blood—makes that consecration a reality. Because when we are in heart brought into oneness with that death, we become not only set apart unto God but separated from every hindrance to our hearkening to the voice of God, to our doing the work of God, to our walking in the will of God. These "members" (Romans 6:13) are not only dedicated, yielded to His service, but because of the separation which the blood effects they are "cleansed" from defilement and also anointed with the oil, the life of the Spirit; they are "meet for the Master's use." The sprinkling with the *blood* and the *oil* puts before us both the *death* and the *life*; which, as we have seen, are needed all along our earthly course.

Hence we see that we need as much the power of Christ's death every day as we do the power of His risen life.

Let us see that we are not seeking to partake of the life without going down into His death. May not our mistakes in the past, and our lack of spiritual vigor, have arisen from failing to see the power of the Cross in the matter of sanctification? Perhaps we have been tempted to think that the death effected our justification only, and that our sanctification was entirely in His life. And this may have led to the idea, more or less prevalent in the minds of many, that having come to the crucified Christ, having seen the Cross in its atoning and justifying aspect, we have now passed beyond it, and have left it behind, because we have entered into living union with the *risen* Christ.

But if we have succeeded in making our meaning intelligible, we now see that this "putting to death of the Lord Jesus"—the essence of His Cross, if we may use the expression—is that which we have to carry about within us always, as an abiding condition of mind, since we need a constant and maintained separation from our old self-life. This is not a matter effected once for all.

His death unto sin has therefore a most important and intimate connection with our practical holiness. The condition of all real progress will consist therefore in the being made conformable to that death. Willingness to die to sin with Christ is a truer evidence of the soul's advance than anxiety to be filled with His life.

It is only thus we are brought to understand the true significance of both baptism and the Lord's Supper. In the one we are buried with Him into death once for all; in the other we become assimilated to that death more and more—we are brought into closer fellowship with the mind of Christ crucified.

The Cross of Christ is therefore not only the place where we find the new life, but also the place where we lose our old life. "The putting to death of the Lord Jesus" was the termination of that life which is "after the flesh," because "our old man"—that is, our old unconverted self—"was crucified with Him." To be brought into oneness with that death, to be so identified with it that we, so to speak, always carry it about, is to be walking in a condition of continual deliverance from the self-life, and to find that the life of Jesus is being manifested in our daily walk.

All spiritual privileges are conditional. The condition of the "life abundant" lies in becoming a partaker of the mind of Him who died unto sin, to be armed with that mind. This is not an isolated experience, a single act, it is a *mind*—that is, a spiritual condition to be ever maintained, and becoming more and more deepened.

We have not, therefore, to strain our energies in order to live, or to increase our strength. The living Christ within us will put forth His own power and manifest His own life; there shall be no lack of vitality. But what we are required to do is voluntarily to submit to die—and this, not by direct efforts upon ourselves but by a participation in us of the mind of Him who died unto sin once and now lives unto God.

The apprehension of the fact that we were identified with Christ when He died on the cross unto sin often produces most sudden and decisive results in the experience and practical walk of the believer. It cuts us away abruptly from our former course of life, and we find a glorious emancipation from sin's power and service. But this effect, though sudden and immediate, is followed by a work which is progressive and continuous. Following the first apprehension of the believer's death with Christ and its results, there is now a deepening work of assimilation of heart and mind to the crucified Christ, a more perfect bringing into sympathy with Him in His death unto sin.

And as this work deepens, as oneness with the dying Christ becomes more and more an experienced reality, so the life increases—the living, risen Lord manifests His power, and fills the soul with His fullness. The believer's true life—that is, the life of Christ in him—is a life, then, that is ever springing up out of death. "I die daily" is a declaration that is fraught with deep meaning, whatever may have been the sense in which the apostle used the words.

It is as we become practically identified with Christ

in His death that all the hindrances to the manifestation of His life are removed. In no other way can they be set aside. Our own efforts cannot accomplish it; our resolutions will utterly fail in effecting it, and leave us in despair.

But God has provided us with a power by which every obstacle may be taken away. That power is the death of Christ. To get the benefit of that power we must submit to be conformed to that death, to be brought into actual sympathy with Him who died unto sin. Just as in the Cross we find the power which sets us free from the authority of darkness and translates us into the kingdom of God's dear Son, so in that death also we possess the power that separates us from the self-life and keeps us in a condition of deliverance.

Taking "the blood of Christ" as equivalent to His death, and the effect of the death to be separation, we can understand how it is that the blood is continually cleansing us from every sin. Walking in the light, as He is in the light, the necessity of this constant separation from sin is felt more deeply continually. But the need is met by God's provision, and we become more and more conscious of the power of that death to separate from sin of every kind; and thence the fellowship between the believer and God is maintained, and becomes a greater reality in his experience.

This gives us another aspect of "the law of liberty" in the spiritual life.

Power belongeth unto God (Psalm 62:11).

Christ the power of God (1 Corinthians 1:24).

The eyes of the LORD run to and fro throughout the whole earth, to show Himself strong in the behalf of them whose heart is perfect toward Him (2 Chronicles 16:9).

And He said unto me, My grace is sufficient for thee: for My strength is made perfect in weakness. Most gladly therefore will I rather glory in my infirmities, that the power of Christ may rest upon me (2 Corinthians 12:9).

That ye may know . . . what is the exceeding greatness of His power to us-ward who believe (Ephesians 1:18–19).

Strengthened with all might, according to His glorious power (Colossians 1:11).

7

CONDITIONS OF POWER

THE ESSENTIAL condition for spiritual power is union with Christ. The power of which we speak is power for practical godliness, personal holiness, and effective service. This power is not from ourselves. It is not something lying dormant within us, something that has been covered up and needs only to be liberated, set free.

It is divine power. Originally God put power into the hands of man, but he lost it at the Fall. Now God has put power in Christ. He does not parcel it out to each one separately, but He has bestowed it on Christ; He has laid it up in His own Son. There it is eternally safe, and there it is for all the members of His body. But while it is there—and there for us!—we cannot have it apart from vital union with Him.

Power is not a *gift* that God bestows. For example, you can communicate the power of a flame to any combustible material, as, for instance, when you light one candle by another. But in that case, the newly lighted candle, whatever the source from which it was lighted, has an independent flame of its own, and burns of itself. Spiritual power is not communicated to the soul after this fashion. It is power by virtue of union.

You go into some large factory; you pass through various departments; in each piece of machinery at work you see power accomplishing marvelous results: and you ask, What sets all these things in motion? Where is the *source* of all this activity?

Then you are taken into the engine-house. There you see the center, the source of all power that is put forth throughout the whole factory. The machinery in each department works not by its own independent force, either generated in itself or originally derived from some other source, but by a force received moment by moment, and continuously, from the central engine.

The essential condition for the communication of the power from the engine to the machinery is union. Break the connection and the power ceases. This is true also of that power which we must have if we are to live overcoming lives. It must be divine power, God's power; not something that has been lying latent in ourselves, not something that we originally derived from God and which is stored up in ourselves, but that which *we are receiving*—which comes to us as a ceaseless stream of energy from the central source of all spiritual life, the Lord Jesus Christ. There must be vital union with Him who is the Power of God.

But we know that all believers are united to Christ, and "he that is joined to the Lord is one spirit." We know also that "if any man have not the Spirit of Christ, he is none of His." So we conclude that a man may hold the doctrine of Christ and yet may not be united to Him; but he cannot have the Spirit of Christ without also having union with Him. The Spirit is the essence of union. This is true of all believers. This union is not a matter of attainment in holiness, it is the starting point of all life, it is the *beginning* of all holiness.

Life comes by receiving the living One. *Identified* with Christ in His atoning *death*, we are *united* to Christ in His risen *life*. "There is one body and there is one Spirit." And the body bears the same name as the Head—"the Christ." "So also is the Christ" (1 Corinthians 12:12). Christ is the Head of angels; but He is the Head of the body, of which every believer is a member, in a far higher sense than He is the Head of angels. They form part of the company of heaven, but believers are members of that body which is the bride of Christ. This union is no figure of speech, no mere dream; it is a reality, literally spiritually true.

Now, however, a difficulty arises. The lack of power which we deplore is in those who are thus united to Christ: how are we to understand this acknowledged deficiency in those who are in vital union with the Source of all power?

Let us in the first place bear in mind that of no believer can it be said absolutely that he has no power. Power, in some measure, every child of God possesses; if there is life there is power. It may be life in its very lowest forms, but if life exists at all there will be some power, however feeble.

But what we now speak of is overcoming power. Not that which simply struggles and offers some resistance to sin, but that which rises triumphantly over every wave of temptation, which is able effectually to withstand every assault of the evil one and courageously to give its witness to the grace, the sufficiency, and the faithfulness of God.

We can understand how there may be union, and yet a lack of power in that sense.

Look at a man whose arm is withered. There is union between the hand and the body; but for all practical purposes there is no power for action or service. Here then we have a figure of the condition of things between many a believer and the Source of all power—union and yet no strength.

This presses the point still nearer home. What are the hindrances that stand in the way of the manifestation of power in those who are in union with Christ? We are all necessarily subject to limitations—limitations that are inseparable from our moral and physical constitution, hindrances that exist in the fact that we are finite creatures.

God's power is infinite, but our capacity is limited. No amount of growth or spiritual progress can so enlarge our capacity that it shall approach equality to God's fullness. There are therefore limitations; but these are not the hindrances to the power of which we speak, these are not the obstacles that have to be removed. While our capacity can never become infinite, it is capable of endless increase—inconceivable expansion. Take, for instance, such passages as these: "All things are possible to him that believeth"; "That ye might be filled with all the fullness of God." The vessel I bring to be filled may be empty, or it may be partly occupied with something else. Worse than all, I may be keeping my hand over its mouth, and thus preventing the water from flowing in. In that case, it is not a question of the sufficiency of supply but of the condition of reception. So even though the provision is infinite and the channel that connects the vessel with the fountain is established—there is union—yet there may be hindrance to the inflowing stream of power. What then is the hindrance?

The great hindrance—that which lies at the root of every other—is *unbelief*. We limit God by our unbelief. The avenues of our being which bring us contact with Christ may become contracted, and the vessel into which the power is to flow may have been reduced to a very small capacity, all through the chilling influences of unbelief. If we are to be filled with the power of God, our faith must grow. Whatever increases our faith will increase our capacity, will open the avenues of our being to God, and the power will flow in.

But instead of looking at power in the abstract, instead of regarding it as a quality we can have *from* God and apart from Him, it will help us to understand the conditions of its manifestation if we think of it as inseparable from the Lord Himself. "The eyes of the LORD run to and fro throughout the whole earth, to show Himself strong in the behalf of them whose heart is perfect toward Him" (2 Chronicles 16:9). Instead of recognizing the truth that I am weak and God is to show *Himself* strong in me, I may be expecting to see myself made strong. I may be looking for an experience of power in myself, rather than for a manifestation of *divine power* in me. He will show *Himself* strong in behalf of him whose heart is perfect towards Him.

The condition of power, then, is to have a perfect heart towards God. What are we to understand by a perfect heart?

Looking at the word in the original we observe first that it means a heart *at peace with God.*

The great work of peace is accepted. "Thou wilt keep him in perfect peace, whose mind is stayed on Thee" (Isaiah 26:3). A heart perfect towards God is a heart that rests on Christ's atoning work. The words "perfect peace," or "peace, peace," include the thought of recompense, thus bringing out the idea of atonement, or the work of peace. The Hebrew word *shalem*, translated as "perfect" in 2 Chronicles 16:9, is rendered as "peaceable" in Genesis 34:21. For when the heart rests on the work of peace—divine, all-sufficient, and completed once for all—it is not only privileged to be at peace *with* God, but to have the peace *of* God; it may know not only the peace of justification but the peace of sanctification. A heart perfect towards God, then, is a heart against which no charge can be laid, which is justified from all things, and also in which there is no longer any controversy with God. The Spirit dwells in such a one not as a Reprover but as a Comforter.

Another thought is suggested by the word *shalem* in that passage in 2 Chronicles. A "perfect" heart is a heart *wholly yielded* to God. We read, "Thou shalt build the altar of the LORD thy God of *whole* stones" (Deuteronomy 27:6. See also Joshua 8:31). Here we have the same word rendered "whole." A perfect heart is a *whole* heart. Wholeness is one of the primary meanings of holiness. Holiness of heart is wholeness of heart. "My son, give Me thine heart" (Proverbs 23:26). A perfect heart is a heart that has responded to that appeal. It gives itself up without reserve. It lays itself wholly on the altar of consecration, and that altar is Christ. The altar consecrates the gift. For "every devoted thing is most holy unto the LORD" (Leviticus 27:28).

But the same word has another rendering. Concerning Solomon's temple it is written, "And the house, when it was in building, was built of stone *made ready* before it was brought thither" (1 Kings 6:7). The word "perfect" is here rendered "made ready." The stones were all prepared and made fit for the builder, they were ready for his use. A perfect heart is therefore a heart in a state of preparedness. It is "meet for the Master's use, and prepared unto every good work" (2 Timothy 2:21). It is "a heart at leisure from itself." Not absorbed in its own cares or spiritual difficulties but being at rest and consecrated to God, it is free to devote itself to His service. As soon as the opportunity presents itself it is ready to embrace it. No time is lost in getting ready. Like an instrument always in tune, such a one is at once prepared to be used by the Master whenever He pleases.

How many spend their time in the work of preparing their hearts, as if their own sanctification were the great end of their calling!

The carpenter sharpens his tools for the work he has to do; but the sharpening of the tools is not the end, but only the means to the end he has in view. So, getting our hearts right with God is only the means toward the accomplishment of the great purposes for which we have been redeemed.

When the artisan who is engaged in some elaborate piece of workmanship requiring the highest skill, the most delicate art, and the best of instruments lays his hand on a tool and then finds that it has lost its edge, he at once lays it down and takes up another that is ready for use. He puts forth his power through those instruments that are perfect or "made ready"; only such is he able to use in his work.

How many of God's children is He obliged to prepare, by severe discipline it may be, before they are meet for His use! How much of pride and self-will and carnal energy have to be taken out of us before we are really fit to be used in His service! It is not from lack of power—power belongs unto God, and there is no lack of power in Him—but from a want of being right towards Him, a want of this perfection of heart of which the Word of God so often speaks, that we know so little of the manifestation of power in ourselves. He is ready and waiting to "show Himself strong in the behalf of him whose heart is perfect toward Him."

Once more, we read concerning David's mighty men that "they came with perfect heart . . . to make David king over all Israel" (1 Chronicles 12:38). There was thorough integrity of heart in the matter. There were no mixed motives, no lack of sincerity. It is a true heart, sincere as the apostle desired in behalf of the Philippians, "that ye may be sincere," that is, "judged in the sunlight and found genuine." It is thorough in its aim and intention—"perfect *toward* God." It describes an *attitude* rather than an *attainment*.

Such a heart does not shrink from divine searching. It willingly yields itself to the penetrating, purifying and consuming power of God's holy fire. Such a heart is loyal toward the Lord; its desire is that Christ should be King over the whole being.

Let this condition of soul be brought about and there will be no lack of power. God Himself will make perfect His strength in our weakness.

How often we have said, "Thine is the power," but how little have we entered into the deep meaning of those words! Too often we have had our minds occupied with the thought, "Oh that mine were the power!" But to have His strength we must have Himself. It is not that He will show that *I* am strong. I am ever to be learning my own weakness—that I am weakness itself. But it is that His strength may overshadow me as a tent. Such is the meaning of the words, ". . . that the power of Christ might rest upon me" (2 Corinthians 12:9).

When God is about to manifest His power through His children, it is thus that He leads them. He brings them into this condition of heart: a condition in which there is no longer any controversy with Him, in which every part of their being is voluntarily yielded to Him, in which the heart is entirely at His disposal and maintained in an attitude of loyalty toward Him. There is then no hindrance in the instrument to the manifestation of His power. The channel is then open, and free from all obstruction to the flowing forth of His fullness. There will then be a manifestation of divine power in all directions.

CONQUERING POWER. The very first enemy that must be conquered, if we would lead triumphant lives, is Self. The only power that can conquer Self is the power of God. We get the benefit of that power by submitting to it—getting under it. To know what it is to be led forth in triumph by Christ you must first become His captive. He is always going forth as the Conqueror, and there are no conquerors but those who are included in His train, who are conquering because conquered by Christ. Have you noticed the reason which the Centurion gave as to why his words commanded obedience? He did not say "Because I am a man *having* authority" but "Because I am a man *under* authority." And the greatness of his faith consisted in this, that he recognized Christ's relationship to the God of heaven. "I *also* am a man under authority." Christ's word was power because He was under divine authority. The centurion recognized Christ's relationship to divine Omnipotence. He thought that just as all the power of Rome was behind him, and he had but to speak and it was done, so all the power of heaven was behind the Man Christ Jesus, and He had but to speak the word only and his servant would be healed.

Here is the secret of reigning over sin. We must be under divine control; we must know what it is fully to submit to it. "Humble yourselves therefore *under the mighty hand of God*."

SUSTAINING POWER. Some there are of God's children who seem to be always struggling to keep themselves up. You see a man in the water. In terror of sinking he begins to struggle, and soon he finds that his struggling is futile, as, in spite of all his efforts, he sinks. But there is power in that very water to keep him afloat. Faith, it is true, is needed, and certain conditions must be fulfilled. One is that he must cease from struggling. Let him cast himself on the water and cease from trying to keep himself from sinking; let him trust the water to bear him up—and instead of sinking he floats!

So it is in finding the power that keeps us spiritually from falling. We must be ready and willing to abandon ourselves to His almighty keeping. The responsibility of keeping us from falling is His; the responsibility of trusting Him to keep us is ours.

PROTECTING POWER. We need this on every hand. Not only over us and under us, but on all sides—encircling us: "who are being guarded in the power of God." Christ, who is the power of God, is the fortress in which the trusting soul is garrisoned. Let the enemy find you thus entrenched and he will be met by a power which is not yours but God's; he cannot touch you. "He that was begotten of God [*i.e.,* Christ] keepeth him, and the evil one toucheth him not" (1 John 5:18, ERV).*

TRANSFORMING POWER. The power of God is to fill us. When the tabernacle was finished, then God's presence filled it. "So Moses finished the work. Then a cloud covered the tent of the congregation, and the glory of the LORD filled the tabernacle. And Moses was not able to enter into the tent of the congregation, because the cloud abode thereon, and the glory of the LORD filled the tabernacle" (Exodus 40:33-35). When we who are the temples of the living God lose the glory, we lose the power. God transforms us by filling us. "That ye might be filled with all the fullness of God" is the blessing the apostle sought on behalf of the Ephesian converts.

Lastly, OVERCOMING POWER. Power, that is, for service, for aggressive work, and for suffering. It is the remark of an able preacher that "the Church has in it a power that is ever adequate to the conquest of the

---

*See also the NIV (ed.).

world" (Maclaren). This is true, because it is God Himself who is in the Church. "God hath said, I will dwell in them, and walk in them" (2 Corinthians 6:16).

When the disciples said to our Lord, after their failure in the matter of the lunatic youth, "Why could not we cast him out?", what was our Lord's answer? "Because of your unbelief." Consecration, the attitude of thoroughness towards God, and faith are closely related.

We are addressing ourselves to those who are believers. It is not therefore a question of the impartation of the gift of faith; it is a question of the exercise of the faith they already possess. How is faith to be increased and strengthened?

There are three things which faith needs: freedom, food, activity.

Faith needs *freedom*. It is thoroughness that liberates faith. When we are brought to give ourselves wholly to the Lord, then it is that our faith is set free. If our eye is not single our faith will be crippled, hampered. "How *can* ye believe which receive honor one of another, and seek not the honor that cometh from God only?" The lack of the single, healthy, undivided eye was that which made faith impossible.

"I feel I cannot trust Him," says one. Why not? Is He not trustworthy? "Oh, yes: but I feel something holding me back." Is it anything like that to which David referred when he said, "If I regard iniquity in my heart, the Lord will not hear me" (Psalm 66:18)? Is there a suspicion that something is withheld? Is there any doubtful thing that you are afraid to bring into the light in order to have God's judgment about it? It is not by "trying to believe" that faith gets strengthened, but by removing the fetters that keep it bound.

Again, faith needs *food*. The Word of God is the food of faith. In order to trust, faith must have something to trust to, a Person to trust in. The Scriptures are the warrant of faith. If faith is not always occupied with this infallible warrant, it will grow weak and feeble. Faith may be suffering from starvation. Our thoughts may turn upon ourselves—we may be occupied with our own activity, with our own act of believing, rather than with the Word of God. But it is only as faith grasps the truth of the Scripture, or the facts that the Scripture reveals, that it gets strengthened.

Once more, faith needs *exercise*. All faith is given to be used. We do not know whether we have it at all until we are using it. This comes out in obedience; for what is obedience but faith in action? Faith must carry out into practice that which it believes.

It is so with the body: unless we take exercise as well as food, we become indolent and slothful. And with the soul there is such a thing as spiritual indigestion. Our practical obedience and courage of faith may be a long way behind our knowledge. Let us be stepping out continually on the light revealed to us—that is, putting into practice, translating into action the truth we are receiving as food into our hearts.

It is as our faith grows that our strength increases. No greater blessing can possibly be desired than the growth of our faith, because this involves the well-being of every other part of our spiritual life.

The apostle said on behalf of the Thessalonians, "We are bound to thank God always for you, brethren, as it is meet, because that your *faith groweth exceedingly*" (2 Thessalonians 1:3).

"According to your faith be it unto you."

Take heed unto yourselves (Deuteronomy 4:23).

Watch ye, stand fast in the faith, quit you like men, be strong (1 Corinthians 16:13).

Watch thou in all things (2 Timothy 4:5).

Praying always with all prayer and supplication in the Spirit, and watching thereunto with all perseverance and supplication for all saints (Ephesians 6:18).

Be ye therefore sober, and watch unto prayer (1 Peter 4:7).

Be sober, be vigilant (1 Peter 5:8).

Be watchful, and strengthen the things which remain, that are ready to die (Revelation 3:2).

8

WATCHFULNESS

THERE are many who feel much perplexity as to the nature of watchfulness and the place it should occupy in the life of the believer. For it must be admitted there is a kind of watchfulness which, instead of being a help, is really a hindrance to the soul in his walk with God because it throws him back upon himself rather than upon Christ, and as a natural result his watching is in vain.

Now it is, of course, with a view of being preserved from sinning, and of being guided aright in our daily life, that watchfulness is needed. But let us first clearly understand that our security does not lie in our ability to keep ourselves. True, our safety is closely bound up with our watching; we *must* watch, and watch continually. But let us never lose sight of the blessed fact that it is the Lord, and He alone, who is our Keeper. "Except the LORD keep the city, the watchman waketh but in vain" (Psalm 127:1).

We must know what it is to be in His keeping before we are in a position to watch. We must be in the Tower, within the Lord's keeping power, before we can really learn what true Christian vigilance means.

Let us clearly recognize the true object of our watching. We may be directing our thoughts and attention in the wrong direction. What is it we have to watch?

Is it the enemy? No, for he has such marvelous powers of deception that he can transform himself into an angel of light. If he had simply *our* vigilance to contend with, *our* power of discernment to cope with, he would have no difficulty in deluding us, for he would find us an easy prey to his subtlety.

There can be but one object of watching: "Looking unto Jesus." There can be no other attitude of watching. And for what do we watch? For the Lord's warnings, His leadings, His teaching.

We have to watch for His *warnings*. It is He who alone sees and knows all Satan's schemes, everything that is going on among the powers of darkness. The believer can see but little of the wiles of the devil; but Christ's omniscient eye penetrates into all the innermost recesses of spiritual wickedness. He can never be taken by surprise. He who never slumbers nor sleeps is ever ready to forewarn His believing followers of all that it is necessary for them to know in order to preserve them from the enemy's power. His loving glance will never fail to put the watching believer on his guard, and acquaint him regarding the enemy's approach, or any special danger that may arise.

And as He can never be taken by surprise, so He never gives a false alarm. No child of God ever fell into grievous sin who had not previously received divine warnings of the approaching danger. The warning neglected was the first step in the fall.

We have to watch for the Lord's *leadings*.

"I will instruct thee and teach thee in the way which thou shalt go: I will guide thee with Mine eye" (Psalm 32:8).

To be guided by God's eye is the most delicate of all kinds of leading. You may guide by your hand someone who is deaf, or you may guide by your voice one who is blind; but you cannot guide one with your eye unless he can see, and is willing to keep his eye on your eye, and understands your looks. But this supposes intimate knowledge, personal acquaintance.

There are many little turnings in the course of the day concerning which we need to know His will, as well as in the great thoroughfares of our journey through life. It is for the silent but unmistakable indications of His eye that we need to be watching if we would abide in His will. How great and momentous are the consequences that sometimes turn upon one trivial event, or that hang upon a single step! Watching is needed not only to be kept from falling into the enemy's snare but to be abiding in the knowledge of God's will.

So if we would know the most blessed, the truest of all kinds of divine leading, we must understand what it is to live so near and to walk with such a vigilant spirit that the eye of God alone is enough to indicate to us what He would have us do and the way He would have us take. There must be a perfect understanding between the soul and Christ.

"Be ye not as the horse, or as the mule, which have no understanding" (Psalm 32:9). True wisdom consists in knowing God's mind. "Be ye not unwise, but understanding what the will of the Lord is" (Ephesians 5:17).

We have to watch for the Lord's *teaching*.

"I will stand upon my watch, and set me upon the tower, and will watch to see what He will say unto me, and what I shall answer when I am reproved" (Habakkuk 2:1). "He wakeneth mine ear to hear as the learned" (Isaiah 50:4). He has many things to teach us which at the early stages of our discipleship we are not able to learn; but He is a wise, gentle, and patient Teacher. We must sit at His feet as Mary did, and learn of Him, not merely by receiving His truth but by partaking of His grace, drinking into His Spirit. He "is full of grace and truth."

"Blessed is the man that heareth Me, watching daily at My gates, waiting at the posts of My doors" (Proverbs 8:34). It is impossible to say how much depends upon this attitude of watching, of hearkening to the voice of the Lord. The best messengers are not those who are the most original, but those who are able the most faithfully to deliver to others what the Lord has spoken to them. It is out of the abundance of the heart that the mouth speaks, but it is by hearkening that the heart is filled. To be good listeners to the voice of the Lord we must know what it is to watch daily at His gates.

Then as to the purpose of our watching. It is with a view to *prayer*. "Watch unto prayer" (1 Peter 4:7). This is an exhortation that occurs frequently. It shows us the immediate purpose for which we are to exercise vigilance.

We shall not watch long before we receive divine indications of the enemy's nearness, and of the necessity of special grace and protection. These times of warnings should be times of prayer—special prayer.

It is not watching alone, then, that is needed, but watching *unto prayer*.

Often the Spirit will prompt us to prayer when, judging from external circumstances, we might be inclined to conclude that no real danger exists, or any special necessity for prayer. But how often have we afterwards discovered—it may be to our cost—that through disregarding the divine call we were betrayed into a snare or overcome by a temptation!

The spirit of vigilance should lead to the deepening and strengthening of the habit of prayer. In answer to the prayer prompted by the Spirit there comes the deliverance, or the relief, or the guidance, or the light sought, as the case may be. This is followed by gratitude and praise. Hence we see the close connection between watching, praying, and thanksgiving, as they so often occur in the Word of God. "Continue in prayer, and watch in the same with thanksgiving" (Colossians 4:2).

Now from what has been said we see that the spirit of watchfulness supposes confidence in Christ's ability, a firm persuasion of His omniscient care and unfailing love. You are no longer questioning His wisdom, His power, or His faithfulness. You can *rest* in His care for you. You can say, "I am persuaded He is *able to keep* that which I have committed unto Him." You are no longer fearful because of the enemy's power, for you know that greater is He that is with you, and in you, than all those that are against you. You can rely on God's keeping power. You know you are on the side of Him who is always triumphant.

But it supposes another thing, and that is a *close*

walk with God. Nearness, not only in worship at certain stated intervals, but in the daily life, throughout each hour of the day. It implies a sensitive conscience—a conscience becoming more and more sensitive to sin's approach, a deeper and truer hatred of its loathsomeness. Not a scrupulous but a healthy, tender conscience—a conscience void of offence.

From this it follows that if I am continually being suddenly overcome by some evil habit, repeatedly taken by surprise by the enemy's assaults, I cannot really be in a spirit of watchfulness. I am not habitually "looking unto Jesus"; I am not walking in fellowship with God. The communication between my soul and the Lord is broken.

We cannot excuse our falls by pleading that we are taken by surprise. We need never be taken by surprise if we are obedient to the warnings which He who knows all things ever gives to those who are watchful.

The following incident will serve to illustrate the important truth we have here touched upon, namely, that the spirit of watchfulness supposes the possession of a sensitive conscience or a faculty of spiritual discernment, which is of the utmost value in our walk of faith.

"In the autumn of 1879, the steamship *Arizona*, 5,000 tons, at that time the swiftest ocean-going steamship in existence, was urging her way at the rate of some fifteen knots on the homeward course from New York, whence she had sailed but a day or two before.

"It was night, and there was a light breeze, but of danger from collision with a passing ship there was little or none. The captain and crew knew of no special reason for watchfulness, and the passengers were altogether free from anxiety.

"Indeed, it so chanced that at a time when, in reality, the most imminent danger threatened every soul on board, many of the saloon passengers were engaged in purchasing at auction the numbers for the next day's run—runs below 350 nautical miles being sold at a very low rate indeed.

"Suddenly a crash was heard. The ship's swift progress was stopped, and a few minutes later everyone knew that the *Arizona* had run dead upon an enormous iceberg, the spires and pinnacles of which could be seen hanging almost over the ship, and gleaming threateningly in the rays of her masthead light.

"But the risk that threatened her living freight was not that of being crushed by falling ice. The bow of the *Arizona* was seen to be slowly sinking, and presently there was a well-marked lurch to starboard. The fore compartment and a smaller side compartment were filling.

"It was an anxious time for all on board. Many an eye was turned towards the boats, and the more experienced thought of the weary miles which separated them from the nearest land, and of the poor chance that a passing steamer might pick up the *Arizona*'s boats at sea.

"Fortunately, the builders of the *Arizona* had done their work faithfully and well. Like another ship of the same line which had been exposed to the same risk, save that her speed was less, and therefore the danger of the shock diminished, the *Arizona*, though crippled, was not sunk. She bore up for St. John's, Newfoundland, and her passengers were taken on later by another steamer.

"The danger which nearly caused the loss of the *Arizona*—collision with an iceberg—is one to which steamships, and especially swift steamships, are exposed in exceptional degree. It is a danger also which makes necessary the duty of careful watching, especially in the night and in times of haze or fog—a most anxious and important care. For, unlike the risk from collision with another ship, the risk from collision with icebergs cannot be diminished by any system of side lights or head lights or stern lights, except in just such degree (unfortunately slight) as a powerful light at the foremast head, aided by strong side lights or bow lights, may serve to render the glance of the treacherous ice discernible somewhat farther ahead. But to a steamship running at a rate of fourteen or fifteen knots, even in the clearest weather, at night the distance athwart at which a low-lying iceberg can be seen, even by the best of eyes, is but short. She runs over it before there is time for the watch to make their warning heard, and for the engineers to stop and reverse their engines.

"But science, besides extending our senses, provides us with senses other than those we possess naturally. The photographic eyes of science see in the thousandth part of a second what our eyes, because in so short a time they can receive no distinct impression at all, are unable to see.

"They may, on the other hand, rest on some faintly luminous object for hours, seeing more and more each moment, where our eyes would see no more—perhaps even less—after the first minute than they had seen in the first second. The spectroscopic eyes of science can analyze for us the substance of self-luminous vapors, or of vapors absorbing light, or of liquids, and so forth, where the natural eyes have no such power of analysis. The sense of feeling, or rather the sense for heat, which Reid originally and properly distinguished as a sixth sense (not to be confounded, as our modern classification of the senses incorrectly confounds it, with the sense of touch), is one which is very limited in its natural range.

"But science can give us eyes for heat as keen and as widely ranging as the eyes which she gives us for light. It was no idle dream of Edison, but a thought which one day will be fraught with useful results, that science may hereafter recognize by its heat a star which the most powerful telescope yet made fails to show by its light. Since that was said, the young Draper (whose loss followed so quickly and so sadly for science on that of his lamented father) has produced photographic plates showing stars which cannot be seen through the telescope by which those photographs were taken. . . . The sense of sight is not the only sense affected as an iceberg is approached. There is a sensible lowering of temperature. But to the natural heat-sense this cooling is not so obvious, or so readily and quickly appreciated that it could be trusted instead of the outlook of the watch.

"The heat-sense of science, however, is so much keener that it could indicate the presence of an iceberg at a distance far beyond that over which the keenest eye could detect an iceberg at night; perhaps even an isolated iceberg could be detected when far beyond the range of ordinary eyesight in the daytime.

"Not only so, but an instrument like the thermopile, or the more delicate heat-measurers of Edison and Langley, can readily be made to give automatic notice of its sensations (so to speak). As those who have heard Professor Tyndall's lectures any time during the last twenty years know, the index of a scientific heat measurer moves freely in response either to gain or loss of heat, or as we should ordinarily say, in response either to heat or cold. An index which thus moves can be made, as by closing or breaking electrical contact, or in other ways, to give very effective indication of the neighborhood of danger.

"It would be easy to devise half a dozen ways in which a heat indicator (which is of necessity a cold indicator), suitably placed in the bow of a ship, could *note*, as it were, *the presence of an iceberg fully a quarter of a mile away*, and speak of its sensations much more loudly and effectively than the watch can proclaim the sight of an iceberg when much nearer at hand. The movement of an index could set a foghorn lustily announcing the approach of danger; could illuminate the ship, if need be, by setting at work the forces necessary for instantaneous electric lighting; could signal the engineers to stop and reverse the engines, or even stop and reverse the engines automatically.

"Whether so much would be necessary—whether those lost Atlantic steamships which have been destroyed, as many have been, by striking upon icebergs, could have been saved only by such rapid automatic measures as these—may or may not be the case, but that the use of the infinitely keen perception which the sense organs of science possess for heat and cold would be a feasible way of obtaining much earlier and much more effective notice of danger from icebergs than the best watch can give, no one who knows the powers of science in this direction can doubt." (Extract from a letter published in *The Times* by Mr. Richard A. Proctor.)

The foregoing statements from the pen of a well-known writer and scientist are deeply interesting, not only as showing the marvelous results of modern scientific discovery but also as illustrating a truth that has its parallel in the spiritual life.

We read, for instance, that among the other blessings conferred upon the believer there is the gift of spiritual discernment. "He hath given us an understanding, that we may know Him that is true" (1 John 5:20). He has "given us a sense" (Lange), so that we are getting to know the True One. The following are Dr. Westcott's remarks on this passage:

"That with which 'the Son of God' incarnate has endowed believers is a power of understanding, of interpreting, of following out to their right issues the complex facts of life; and the end of the gift is that they may know, not by one decisive act, but by a continuous and progressive apprehension, 'Him that is true.'"

This then is a real endowment, of which those who are watchful and are walking in obedience to God's leading are made really conscious. They have given to them "the power of believing in and seeing, little by little, the divine purpose of life under the perplexing riddles of phenomena."

In words that are scarcely figurative, we may say

with truth that with the approach of some special forms of temptation or peril *"there is a sensible lowering of temperature."* We are made conscious that danger is at hand by something we cannot describe or explain; we feel that a call to special vigilance and prayer has come to us from above. Such warnings cannot be neglected without serious loss. Let them be the occasion of a steadier gaze, of a simpler trust, of a humbler dependence, of a more childlike confidence in God, and of a prompt obedience.

This faculty of spiritual discernment is not a gift to be lightly esteemed. It cannot be trifled with; it may be easily obscured or entirely lost through want of watchfulness or careless walking. And when lost, it is not so easily restored.

Few gifts are more precious than this faculty of spiritual eyesight, or the sense by which any lowering of the moral temperature may be at once detected. Often it will be the means of keeping us from venturing into scenes where the Spirit of God would be grieved, and where not only our joy and peace but our liberty and power in service are forfeited.

On the other hand, the gift is strengthened by use and becomes more and more sensitive. We grow in the possession of an "understanding heart." And as we live in this watchful and obedient attitude we are brought to know, in a way that no commentary could teach us, the meaning of these words of the apostle: "That ye might be filled with the knowledge of His will in all wisdom and spiritual understanding; that ye might walk worthy of the Lord unto all pleasing, being fruitful in every good work, and increasing in the knowledge of God" (Colossians 1:9–10).

Fight the good fight of faith (1 Timothy 6:12).

Now thanks be unto God, which always causeth us to triumph in Christ [or, who at all times is leading us in triumph in Christ] (2 Corinthians 2:14).

In all these things we are more than conquerors through Him that loved us (Romans 8:37).

Thanks be to God, which giveth us the victory through our Lord Jesus Christ (1 Corinthians 15:57).

Finally, my brethren, be strong in the Lord, and in the power of His might. Put on the whole armour of God, that ye may be able to stand against the wiles of the devil (Ephesians 6:10–11).

Walk in the Spirit, and ye shall not fulfil the lust of the flesh (Galatians 5:16).

9

CONFLICT

ALMOST immediately after the believer realizes what it is to have eternal life in Christ he is brought face to face with conflict. It is of the utmost importance that he should understand clearly the principles on which the warfare is to be waged, and what are the essential conditions to be maintained in order that there should be not just conflict, but *victorious* conflict.

One of the chief passages of Scripture on this important subject is the sixth chapter of the Epistle to the Ephesians.

The first thing to be noticed is the *preparation* for the battle. This is given us in the tenth verse: "Be strong in the Lord, and in the power of His might." When the apostle put before us the Christian life under the figure of a race, he showed us what are the needful qualifications in order to run so as to obtain the prize; now, when he speaks of this conflict, he lays down the preliminary condition which is essential in order that we may come off conquerors: We must know what it is to become strengthened in the Lord.

The apostle addresses himself to those who have already apprehended their judicial standing in Christ. It is not now a question of salvation, but of becoming empirically and practically strengthened, of which he here speaks. It is something that he presses upon them as that which is absolutely essential for Christian conflict.

But how is the exhortation to be obeyed? To be made powerful in the Lord is to occupy a certain position from which alone the battle can be successfully waged. In order to do this we must first see clearly the nature of the victory the Lord Jesus Christ has obtained for His people.

He is not only the Mediator between God and man, He is the Conqueror of our great spiritual adversary. He has not only atoned for our sins by His merits, He has overcome our foes by His almighty power. Through His death He has vanquished him who had the power of death, that is, the devil; He has triumphed over every enemy that can possibly assail us. When God raised Christ from the dead and set Him at His own right hand, it was "far above all principality, and power, and might, and dominion, and every name that is named, not only in this world, but also in that which is to come: and hath put all things under His feet" (Ephesians 1:21–22). To be strengthened in the Lord we must first see Him as the Conqueror; we must see Him occupying the victorious position.

As has often been observed, the Epistle to the Ephesians in the New Testament answers to the Book of Joshua in the Old. It is in the Book of Joshua that the Lord manifests Himself as a man of war. In Exodus He

reveals Himself as the Redeemer, but it is not until the
children of Israel are standing within the borders of the
promised land that Jehovah appears to them as the
Conqueror: "As the Captain of the LORD's host am I
now come." It is the same divine Person, but a new
revelation; it is the same Lord, but a fresh manifestation. They had only just placed their feet on true fighting ground; to lead them forth to the conflict and to
teach them the true secret of victory does He now
come.

A full view of the Captain, and a clear apprehension
of the complete victory He has already obtained, is the
first step towards becoming strong in the Lord and in
the power of His might.

But the next step is to identify ourselves with Him in
His victory. What did Joshua require the captains of his
men of war to do? Not simply to take in the fact that he
had conquered the five kings whom he had placed in
the cave, but also to identify themselves with him in the
victory. As representatives of the camp of Israel they
were required to place their feet on the necks of these
kings (Joshua 10:24).

So *our* Joshua would have His believing followers
not only to recognize the fact that He has triumphed
over the foe, but also by faith to plant their feet on that
victorious position which He has obtained for them. He
would have us enter into His triumphs, into the fruits of
His conquest—not only to stand in His righteousness,
but by faith to claim and occupy the victorious position
in relation to all our foes. This is to be made powerful
in the Lord and in the strength of His might.

Now let it be clearly understood that to occupy the

victorious position as a preparation for battle is not a question of progressive attainment but a matter of immediate acceptance by faith. We take it *before* we begin to fight, for not until that position is taken are we prepared for the conflict.

It is a position superior to that of the enemy. Christ does not bring the believer into the valley while the enemy is occupying the heights. The conflict does not consist in obtaining the victory with His aid, and dislodging the enemy from his vantage ground. The character of the conflict is entirely different. To see what Christ has accomplished by *His* victory is to see that the enemy has already been overcome and dislodged from his stronghold, and that our conflict consists in fighting not *for* this position of victory but *from* it. We are to fight not in order to reach the place of victory, but, occupying that position in Christ, being strengthened in Him, we fight *from* it. The essence of the conflict is not to go up and *take* possession, but to stand *in* possession. Because possession is taken the moment we stand in Christ, what we then have to do is to hold our ground. We have to "keep the field," as Martin Luther puts it. And so the apostle uses this expression, "that ye may be able to withstand, . . . and having done all, to stand" (Ephesians 6:13).

But again, the preparation for the battle includes another essential condition. Not only must the right position be occupied; the equipment which God has provided must be appropriated—"put on."

"Put on the whole armour of God." Here again the words must be understood not as having reference to our judicial standing—for this could not be a matter of exhortation—but to our practical conduct. The apostle refers to that which has to be appropriated. Without entering in detail into the meaning of this armor, we may point out in passing that what we have here is equivalent to the direction given by the same apostle in his Epistle to the Romans: "Put ye on the Lord Jesus Christ" (Romans 13:14). We may sum it up by saying that to put on Christ is to be brought into entire subjection to His supremacy, to be wholly under His control. This, as we have seen in another chapter, is the secret of having His power. Until this is actually brought about we are not ready to engage in the battle.

In the next place, observe the foe to be encountered. The enemy especially referred to in the sixth chapter of the Epistle to the Ephesians is not the world or the flesh, but Satan. "For we wrestle not against flesh and blood, but against principalities, against powers, against the rulers of the darkness of this world, against spiritual wickedness in high [or, heavenly] places." That is, we are not fighting against mankind. It is not against the human instruments but against Satan himself, who is employing these instruments, that we wage war. The real enemy is not visible to the outward eye. He is an unseen but mighty foe; he is behind and underneath all that is visible and human and physical. The enemy here contemplated, therefore, is not an internal but an external foe.

Now it may be objected, Is not the "flesh" an enemy? and is not the "flesh" within us? True. But let us not fail to observe that if the preparation for the battle has really been carried out, if the preliminary conditions have been complied with, then the flesh is no longer free to hinder us. That tendency to evil which continues with us to the last is no longer in power but is held in subjection by the supremacy of Christ.

The fight does not consist in an internal conflict. This would be mutiny. The believer cannot really conquer himself; but by giving Christ the throne, by simply falling in with His conditions, self is conquered—the flesh is held in abeyance, kept in the place of death—so that the believer is free to fight the enemies of the Lord.

We must very jealously distinguish between rebellion and true Christian conflict. If we are not willing that God should have His way with us, if we are setting up our will in opposition to His will, this certainly is conflict; but it is not Christian conflict, it is not "the good fight of faith." It is like a soldier who, going out to fight his country's enemy, is found during the progress of the battle sometimes on the side of the foe, fighting in his ranks against his own country, and at other times in the ranks of his own army. Unless we are really on the Lord's side, truly loyal to Him, we are not engaged in the warfare described in this epistle.

The believer who really fulfills the conditions insisted upon in the tenth and following verses in this sixth chapter of the Epistle to the Ephesians is, as Gurnal says, a *"Christ-enclosed man."* Satan knows what that means better than we do. He is too experienced a general to waste his strength against walls which he knows are impregnable. So he does not come against us with his power when we are thus entrenched; he adopts other methods. He brings his "wiles" to bear upon us—his subtle, methodized plans—in order to allure us out of our Stronghold. The apostle speaks of

them as "the wiles of the devil." His aim is to get the
believer to quit faith's position. If he can only get him
to doubt, or even to entertain discouragement—for all
discouragement comes from the devil—he will succeed
in his schemes; for the moment the believer quits faith's
position he falls under Satan's power. Hence the fight
is not merely "the good fight" (good because it may
always be a victorious one), but "the good fight of
faith," because it is essentially a question of maintain-
ing the trusting attitude and remaining in faith's position.

It should encourage the weakest believer to remember that the "babe in Christ" who is *within* the impregnable Fortress is as safe as the "father in Christ" who
occupies the same position; but the most advanced saint
is as weak and helpless as water the moment he ceases
to abide in the Fortress and have Christ between himself and the enemy.

The order in which the several pieces are enumer-
ated is the order in which the armor of the Roman
soldier was actually put on. And being armed, the soldier had then only to take up the sword or the spear.
Now it is curious to note that St. Paul omits the *spear*;
but this is exactly that part of his equipment which
when on guard *within the fortress* the soldier would not
be likely to assume.

Lastly, observe the result to be expected in this conflict. There are three "ables" in this passage that should
be carefully noted. The first is in verse 11, "That ye
may be able to stand against the wiles of the devil." The
provision made for us in the armor is sufficient to
enable us to stand. There is no reason why even the

weakest saint should be overcome by Satan. It is God's purpose that we should come off victorious. Let us expect not defeat but triumph. How often have we been defeated because we have gone into the conflict anticipating failure!

The next "able" is in verse 13; but notice first the one in verse 16: "Above all, taking the shield of faith, wherewith ye shall be able to quench all the fiery darts of the wicked." Let us not overlook the little word "*all*." We know something of these fiery darts and the suffering they occasion: those unbelieving thoughts, desponding, hard, abominable thoughts—inflaming our worst passions and plunging us into the darkest gloom. How we long to be delivered! Well, here is God's warrant for our confident expectation that we may be. Where is the remedy? It is in the shield of faith. Let that shield be ever between us and the enemy, and not a single dart shall reach our souls. "All the fiery darts of the wicked" shall be quenched.

Christ is the shield that faith apprehends. Let Him stand between you and the foe, and you need fear no evil. This invisible and impenetrable shield shall surround you on every side and guard you from every assault.

In the thirteenth verse we read, "That ye may be able to withstand in the evil day, and having done all, to stand." This expression, "withstand," occurs also in the Epistle of James, "Resist [*i.e.,* withstand] the devil, and he will flee from you" (James 4:7); and also in the First Epistle of Peter, "Whom resist [withstand] steadfast in the faith" (1 Peter 5:9). The King James Version might lead us perhaps to the idea that the believer's duty was to go out and encounter the enemy, and seek to overcome him by dint of his own power of resistance; but bearing in mind that the word is really "withstand," we see at once that the only way in which Satan can successfully be encountered is for us to be found by him entrenched in Christ. The only way we can "resist" him is for us to stand in Christ our Fortress, and to meet his assaults with Christ as our wall of defense. So is that passage in First Peter to be understood. We are to "resist" Satan by being steadfast in the faith; that is, by standing fast in faith's victorious position.

All these passages enable us to see clearly that the conflict is indeed a fight of *faith*, and also to detect the secret of our past failures. We have not seen the indispensable necessity of this attitude of trust; we have relied on our own efforts, our own resolutions, our own prayers, it may be. While we have believed that justification was by faith, we have not really believed that the fight and the victory were also to be known and realized through faith. But this is God's appointed means. Let us not make experiments by using any other method.

"The law of liberty" is nowhere more necessary to our spiritual success than in this matter of conflict. If we are not really free from ourselves, we cannot fight so as to "withstand." Too much stress cannot, therefore, be laid on the tenth and following verses. *There* lies the secret of a continuous life of triumph over the power of the enemy.

How David anticipated the great truth set forth in this chapter we see from what he says in the eighteenth psalm:

The LORD is my rock, and my fortress, and my deliverer; my God, my strength, in whom I will trust; my buckler, and the horn of my salvation, and my high tower. . . .

It is God that girdeth me with strength, and maketh my way perfect.

He maketh my feet like hinds' feet, and setteth me upon my high places.

He teacheth my hands to war, so that a bow of steel is broken by mine arms.

Thou hast also given me the shield of Thy salvation: and Thy right hand hath holden me up, and Thy gentleness hath made me great. . . .

For Thou hast girded me with strength unto the battle: Thou has subdued under me those that rose up against me.

Thou hast also given me the necks of mine enemies. . . .

Therefore will I give thanks unto Thee, O LORD, among the heathen, and sing praises unto Thy name (vss. 2, 32-35, 39–40, 49).

But an important passage as bearing on this subject of conflict has not yet been noticed. It is the well-known declaration which the apostle gives us in his Epistle to the Galatians: "But I say, Walk by the Spirit, and ye shall not fulfil the lust of the flesh. For the flesh lusteth against the Spirit, and the Spirit against the flesh; for these are contrary the one to the other; that ye may not do the things that ye would. But if ye are led by the Spirit, ye are not under the law" (Galatians 5:16–18, ASV).

It is of the utmost moment, in order to understand the meaning of these words, that we have clearly before us what the apostle here means by "the Spirit." There are multitudes of Christians who read the words as if we have here described *the struggle between the two natures*, flesh and spirit. Let us once and for ever dismiss that thought from our minds in connection with this text. This is not the teaching of the passage. The apostle by the term "Spirit" here does not refer to the human spirit, that which is a part of every man's constitution; nor does he here speak of the new nature, "that which is born of the Spirit." As Alford observes on this text, Spirit here is "not man's spiritual part; it is (as in verse 5) the Holy Spirit of God." So to the same effect another well-known commentator has remarked: "Spirit is here doubtless the Holy Ghost; it is that that overcomes the flesh. He enters, it is true, into the hearts of believers, and works only by impelling and determining the walk, as He who dwells in the believers. But yet 'Spirit' [here] is not on this account equivalent to the new disposition of the believer himself, sanctified by the Spirit, but remains ever distinct from the individual human spirit, as Divine, transcending it" (Lange).

This moreover is clear from the context. To "walk in the Spirit" is to walk in the Holy Spirit. "The fruit of the Spirit" (verse 22) is the fruit of the Holy Spirit, not of our new nature. So here what the apostle declares is the opposition between the flesh and the Holy Spirit—the Holy Spirit being here regarded not so much as working externally on the believer, but as an indwelling Power.

What the apostle here declares is that "walking in the Holy Spirit" is the means of living in continual triumph over, or in a state of deliverance from, the "lust of the flesh."

The enemy which the apostle has now especially in view is not Satan—the conflict in that relation we have already considered in connection with the sixth of Ephesians—but here it is the flesh. We must ask, however, What does the apostle mean here by the "flesh"?

We know the term is used in Scripture to denote man-kind generally: "All flesh is as grass." It is also used of our physical nature, our bodily organism: "The life that I now live in the flesh." But there is another sense in which the word is used, and especially by the Apostle Paul. The flesh is spoken of as the seat of sin. "The expression gives us no right whatever to think of the bodily organism more than of the soul" (Lange). It must not be taken as equivalent to our material or physical nature. "The essential element in the idea of the flesh is the *turning away from God* and referring ourselves to ourselves, the *self-seeking*, egoistic element. This is primarily in respect to God, but immediately connected with it is the fact that in reference to other men a man also seeks himself, his enjoyment or his gain. It is easily explicable therefore why love appears as the first effect of the Spirit, being the temper and act opposed to selfishness" (Muller on "The Christian Doctrine of Sin," quoted in Lange's *Commentary*).

Selfhood is the essence of that principle called the "flesh." The flesh is that *tendency* to self or to sin which exists even in the regenerate. Adam was created origi-nally without this evil tendency, though he had the *liability* to sin. But we must not overlook the distinction between the *tendency* and the *liability* to sin. A piece of wood floating on the water has no tendency to sink. It is liable to sink, because it may be submerged by external pressure. But a piece of lead floating on the water by means of a life belt, though it does not actually sink, has a tendency of its own to sink.

Now we believe that the "flesh," however it may be defined, is that which is incapable of being turned into spirit. And we believe, moreover, that the Scripture teaches us that it will exist in the believer as a tendency to evil to the last; that is, that it is not in this life actually eradicated. Therefore we need a power greater than that we possess by nature, greater than that we possess *in ourselves* by grace, a power which is divine, even the Holy Spirit Himself, to meet that tendency and continually give us deliverance from it. We need continually the exercise of that divine power which "is able to keep us from falling." And we may always have it; so that, though the tendency to sink is not removed, it is effectually counteracted.

The two principles are diametrically opposed. But, as Lange observes, "the contest" described in this passage (Galatians 5:16–18) "is by no means to be conceived as an interminable one. The context shows that on the contrary there is expected of the Christian a complete surrendering of himself, *in order to be actuated by the one principle, the Spirit, and a refusal to give way to the lust of the flesh.*"

What then is needed on the part of the believer in order that his life may be a life of triumph? Not struggles with the flesh to overcome it. He has no power really to conquer the flesh; but he is free to choose either the flesh or the Spirit. He can yield either to the one or the other; and by the constant surrender of his will to the Holy Spirit, he finds at once that power in God which he does not possess in himself, a power that completely conquers the flesh and gives him continually a path of deliverance from its lusts. And hence the result is *we do not the evil things* we otherwise should inevitably do if the Holy Spirit were not in us. But note what the apostle says at the end of this chapter: "They that are of Christ Jesus have crucified the flesh with the passions and the lusts thereof" (vs. 24, ASV).

"The meaning, to be sure, is not that now the flesh, with its affections and lusts, is not any longer present at all with those that have become Christians." Crucifixion, here, "naturally alludes to the cross of Christ, and the fellowship with Christ involves a crucifixion of the flesh, for the very reason that it is fellowship with Christ's *death* on the cross." Those, therefore, who appropriate to themselves in faith Christ's death upon the cross "*have divested themselves of all vital fellowship with sin*, whose seat the 'flesh' is, so that as Christ was objectively crucified, we, by means of the entrance into fellowship of His death on the cross, crucify the flesh subjectively, in moral consciousness of faith." That is, have made it "inoperative through faith as the new vital element to which we have passed over. To Christians considered *ideally*, as here, this ethical slaying of the flesh is something which *has* taken place; in *reality*, however, it is also something *taking place* and *continuing*" (Lange).

What we have already said on the subject of "conformity to the death of Christ," in another chapter, bears on this point. It is our identification with *Christ's death unto sin*, and being made one with Him in mind and heart in that death, that not only brings the flesh to the cross but *keeps* it there. To keep it in the place of death is the only way to walk in a path of continual deliverance.

It is in and through and by the *Spirit* then that this mortifying or putting to death of the flesh is to be accomplished (Romans 8:13), and this only by means of the cross.

What, therefore, this chapter of the Epistle to the Galatians puts before us is not a description of that struggling between the two natures which so many Christians mistake for true Christian warfare, but the way of deliverance from one of our most serious hindrances to victorious conflict. It shows us how by the power of the Holy Spirit we may stand in a position of freedom from the harassing influences of the "lust of the flesh"—a freedom which is essential in order that we may engage in the conflict, run in the race, labor in the work, and abide in the fellowship to which by God's grace we have been called.

Ye shall receive power, when the Holy Spirit is come upon you (Acts 1:8, ASV).

They were all filled with the Holy Ghost (Acts 2:4).

Therefore being by the right hand of God exalted, and having received of the Father the promise of the Holy Ghost, He hath shed forth this, which ye now see and hear (Acts 2:33).

At that day ye shall know that I am in My Father, and ye in Me, and I in you (John 14:20).

Be filled with the Spirit (Ephesians 5:18).

And the very God of peace sanctify you wholly: and I pray God your whole spirit and soul and body be preserved blameless unto the coming of our Lord Jesus Christ. Faithful is He that calleth you, who also will do it (1 Thessalonians 5:23–24).

10

FILLED WITH THE HOLY SPIRIT

MANY of God's children have been aroused to
seek afresh that power for service with which
the Holy Spirit alone can clothe them. They have found
in their experience that the blessings realized at their
conversion have by no means exhausted the "riches"
treasured up for them in Christ; and that the fresh needs
that have sprung up in their path, since first they set out
to follow the Lord, cannot be satisfied by the fact
(blessed though it be) that, "being justified by faith, we
have peace with God through our Lord Jesus Christ."

They have seen that though, like the Ephesian converts, they have understood what it is to "have redemption through His blood, the forgiveness of sins, according to the *riches of His grace*," still there is for them the
further blessing which the apostle sought on behalf of
these converts in the words, "that He would grant you,
according to the *riches of His glory*, to be strengthened
with might by His Spirit in the inner man; that Christ
may dwell in your hearts by faith; that ye, being rooted
and grounded in love, may be able to comprehend with
all saints what is the breadth, and length, and depth, and

height; and to know the love of Christ, which passeth knowledge, that ye might be filled with all the fulness of God" (Ephesians 3:16–19).

Very many have had their minds more or less exercised touching the blessing of the "baptism of the Holy Spirit," as it is often termed. We believe not a few have been hindered, if not actually thrown back in their spiritual course, simply for lack of a little instruction in the very first principle of the doctrine concerning the Person, offices, and work of the Holy Spirit.

The first point to be recognized, as clearly set forth in the Scriptures, is the fact that all Christians have the Holy Spirit. They have not only been brought under His influence, they have received the Holy Spirit Himself. "If any man have not the Spirit of Christ, he is none of His" (Romans 8:9). "It is remarkable," observes Professor Godet, "that the Spirit of Christ is here used as the equivalent of the Spirit of God in the preceding proposition. The Spirit of Jesus is that of God Himself, whom He [Jesus] has converted by appropriating Him perfectly here below into His personal life, so that He can communicate Him to His own. It is in this form that the Holy Spirit henceforth acts in the Church. Where this vital bond does not exist between a soul and Christ, it remains a stranger to Him and His salvation." At the same time we must recognize the fact that to *have* the Spirit is one thing, but to be *filled* with the Spirit is quite another thing. We know from what is recorded in John's Gospel (20:22) that even before the Ascension the Holy Spirit had actually been given to the disciples, that Christ breathed upon them the Holy Spirit. But on the day of Pentecost they were *filled* with the Holy

Spirit.

A careful study of the New Testament scriptures with a view to an understanding of what is said of the fullness of the Spirit has led us to notice four distinct ways in which men were filled with the Holy Spirit.

FIRST. After a season of waiting. This is recorded in the first chapter of the Acts of the Apostles. The disciples had a distinct promise to rest on, and a definite direction to obey. The promise was, "Ye shall be baptized with the Holy Ghost not many days hence" (Acts 1:5). The command or direction was that they should not depart from Jerusalem, but "wait for the promise of the Father, which, saith He, ye have heard of Me" (Acts 1:4; also Luke 24:49). After this season of waiting, there came the filling we read of in the second chapter of the Acts: "They were all *filled* with the Holy Ghost" (Acts 2:1–4).

SECOND. After a season of prayer. "And when they had prayed, the place was shaken where they were assembled together; and they were all *filled* with the Holy Ghost, and spake the word of God with boldness" (Acts 4:31). We must not fail to observe that the words here used are precisely those we have in Acts 2:4. The repetition of the phrase seems to teach us that even the apostles themselves needed the continual renewal of the Holy Spirit. They were not resting on a past experience, nor depending on the provision received at Pentecost. The blessing they received then brought them into the attitude of looking up to the risen Lord for "the supply of the Spirit of Jesus Christ" (Philippians 1:19). What we have here recorded in this fourth chapter of the Acts teaches us also that the wonderful blessings of

Pentecost did not make them independent of prayer.

THIRD. After the laying on of hands. "Then laid they their hands on them, and they received the Holy Ghost" (Acts 8:17). And again: "When Paul had laid his hands upon them, the Holy Ghost came on them; and they spake with tongues, and prophesied" (Acts 19:6).

FOURTH. After preaching, or during the very act of proclaiming the gospel. "*While* Peter yet spake these words, the Holy Ghost fell on all them which heard the word" (Acts 10:44). "And *as I began* to speak, the Holy Ghost fell on them, as on us at the beginning" (Acts 11:15). The italics are not in the original, but we emphasize the words to show that it was during the time the word was being preached that the blessing came.

From these facts we see that men were filled with the Spirit in more than one way, and that it is not correct to conclude that unless there has been a season of waiting with this definite object, the particular blessing here referred to cannot be received.

Another point which is instructive to note, in connection with the events recorded in the Acts, is the distinction between being "full" and being "filled." The first indicates an abiding or habitual condition, the latter a special inspiration or inflowing—a momentary action or impulse of the Spirit for service, at particular occasions.

These passages should be carefully noted.

We read, for instance, "Wherefore, brethren, look ye out among you seven men of honest report, *full* of the Holy Ghost and wisdom. . . . And they chose Stephen, a man full of faith and of the Holy Ghost" (Acts 6:3–5), etc. And again, touching Barnabas, "For he was a good man, and *full* of the Holy Ghost and of faith" (Acts 11:24).

The word "full" in these passages denotes the abiding characteristic—these were men who had been filled and were habitually *full* of the Holy Ghost.

But for special service—times of need and occasions of peculiar difficulty or trial—this was not enough. To those thus full there came additional or special supplies, which caused them to overflow. There was, so to speak, a welling up of the spring within. Compare John 4:14 with John 7:38.

Thus we read, "Then Peter, filled with the Holy Ghost" (Acts 4:8), etc. He who was already full received there and then a fresh filling. And again, "Then Saul (who is also called Paul), *filled* with the Holy Ghost," etc. The word here points to a sudden inflowing for a special occasion.

Now what believers should seek, or claim as that which is their privilege, is the habitual condition—always to be full of the Spirit.

This does not necessarily suppose any wonderful experience of joy, ecstasy, or consciousness of power; but a sense of nearness, of childlike confidence, of constant and entire dependence on the Lord. It gives us a sense of His indwelling.

If we are "full of the Holy Ghost" we shall find, as special difficulties arise, and special calls for service come to us, that there will always be that "filling," or momentary supply, which will enable us to triumph, to witness, to serve, or to bring forth fruit, as the case may be, according to His will. And it is when these fillings come that we overflow.

This abiding condition of being full of the Spirit should characterize every child of God at all times and in all circumstances. It is not a privilege that belongs only to a favored few, nor is it something to be expected only at certain seasons and under peculiar circumstances.

The normal condition of the believer may be illustrated by a vessel filled with water to the brim. This does not render him independent of further supplies, nor does it make him self-satisfied. On the contrary, to be thus "full" is to be conscious of one's own utter insufficiency, and the necessity of God's sustaining and renewing grace, moment by moment. It is the soul who is "full of the Holy Ghost" who really looks up, and trusts with childlike simplicity for the momentary supply.

These "fillings" come just when God sees they are needed; and then it is that the soul overflows with those "rivers of living water" which our Lord declared should be the characteristic of Pentecostal days.

But the experience of so many of God's children is often sadly different. While they may know what it is at certain times to receive the fullness, and for a season to be "full of the Holy Ghost," so great and subtle is the spiritual *leakage* that, too commonly, it is not long before they relapse into a condition of emptiness, which renders them unfit for the Master's use. Though they may find that special times of need, and of service, are met by special supplies, they no longer find that with these supplies there are also the overflowings. And the reason is obvious. The high-water mark of their spiritual life, so to speak, is far below the level of their own capacity.

Now it is clear that what is needed is, first, to be made "full," and then to abide in that fullness. The "fillings" will come in the path of service according to our need. We need not be anxious about receiving the momentary supplies. God will fill to the full all our need, "according to His riches in glory by Christ Jesus."

This blessing of being made "full" is ordinarily realized in connection with three things—waiting, desiring, and receiving.

Waiting. We would not say that the fullness of the Spirit can be known only after a season of waiting, for we have it recorded in Acts 10:44 that "*while* Peter yet spake these words, the Holy Ghost fell on all them which heard the word." There had been no tarrying for this special gift, no definite expectation had been awakened; but suddenly, while they listened to the gospel message, they were endued with the Holy Ghost. That St. Peter recognized the blessing as identical with that which the apostles themselves received at Pentecost we learn from the 47th verse, "Can any man forbid water, that these should not be baptized, *which have received the Holy Ghost as well as we?*"

Still, we know that one of the divinely appointed means by which our spiritual strength is renewed is that of waiting on the Lord.

We have to wait, not because He is not ready to bless—He waits to be gracious—but in order that we may be made ready to receive His blessing.

An essential condition of all spiritual progress and power is soul-rest. The believer must know what it is to enter into God's rest if he would be filled with His

Spirit. This is one of the chief purposes of waiting. We wait *on* the Lord—attentive to His wishes as a waitress to those of her customer—rather than *for* the Lord. And as we wait He prepares the vessel He is about to fill, by bringing it into a state of stillness before Him.

It is a rest that comes from casting all our cares upon Him. If, instead of bringing them to the Lord, laying them upon Him and leaving them there, we are carrying them, we shall fail to comply with the primary condition of being filled with the Spirit. But if, as we wait on the Lord, we let down our burdens and lay aside every weight, we then take the first steps that lead to this blessed result.

It is a rest that comes from ceasing from self. This brings us into a still deeper experience of tranquility. By this means the adjustment of our inner being is brought about. This is to exchange our strength. "They that wait on the LORD shall renew [change] their strength" (Isaiah 40:31). The Lord Himself, instead of our renewed nature, becomes the center of our activity. Then it is we learn the true meaning of self-denial, which is to ignore oneself, and to know no other but Christ as the source of our life.

It is a rest that comes from submitting to God in everything. By waiting we get down; we humble ourselves under the mighty hand of God; we get under His power, under His control. Then it is that we become like the clay in the hand of the potter; then it is that all self-energy and eagerness and anxiety cease, and the whole being is surrendered unreservedly into the hands of God that He might work in us "that which is well-pleasing in His sight through Jesus Christ."

Desiring. Faith sees that to be "full of the Holy Ghost" is a blessing not peculiar to apostolic days but the great privilege of every believer in the present dispensation, that it is a blessing which may be now known and realized, and that to live without this "fullness" is to live below our true normal condition.

Let this be seen and felt, and at once a desire is awakened in the soul which is the forerunner of the blessing itself. Without this desire our prayers for the Spirit's fullness would be cold, formal, and unreal. The longing to be filled is often brought about by a painful sense of barrenness of soul. Language like that of David in Psalm 63:1 is felt to be the exact expression of the soul's desire after the life and freshness which God alone can bestow: "My flesh longeth for Thee in a dry and thirsty land, where no water is." How many a Christian is in this "desert land" as to his experience! It is sad indeed to be in such a condition, but more sad to be barren and unfruitful and yet have no longings for the "water brooks." Is not this the secret of the Church's weakness today—dry, barren and unfruitful, and yet little or no real desire to be "filled with the fullness of God"?

But when God is about to fill the soul He allures her into the "wilderness" (Hosea 2:14). He brings her to see and feel her need. It is "from thence" that He causes her to receive "the fullness of blessing." To be brought to know one's parched and barren condition is to see the utter folly and sin of all worldly compromise, and the necessity of a full and complete surrender to God. We are no longer shrinking from the thought of being too "out and out" for God, or of losing too much of this world's treasures. We are no longer afraid of going all lengths with God; we are now willing that He should have His own way with us.

Have you, my reader, been brought to this point of self-despair? Have you been brought to know by bitter experience that a half-hearted life brings us, sooner or later, to "a thirsty land where no water is"?

Thank God if now the language of your heart is that of David's: "As the hart panteth after the water brooks, so panteth my soul after Thee, O God. My soul thirsteth for God, for the living God" (Psalm 42:1–2). This desire, let us observe, is not for God's gifts merely, but for God Himself—"the living God."

The same intense longing of soul after the presence and fullness of the Lord Himself is expressed in another psalm: "I stretch forth my hands unto Thee: my soul thirsteth after Thee, as a thirsty land" (Psalm 143:6).

Now we know that to this spirit of desire itself a blessing belongs. Our Lord gave it a beatitude. "Blessed are they which do hunger and thirst after righteousness: for they shall be filled." Still, let us not stop at the desire. The "thirsting" is only the preparation for the "filling." This brings us to the . . .

Receiving. While we plead God's promises, let us not forget to obey His commands. "Receive ye the Holy Ghost," "Be filled with the Spirit," are divine commands. When Peter and John came to the Christian converts at Samaria, they "prayed for them that they might *receive* the Holy Ghost" (Acts 8:15). When Paul came to Ephesus and found there certain disciples, he put this question to them, "Did ye receive the Holy Spirit when ye believed?" (Acts 19:2, ASV). Quite apart from the question as to what kind of disciples these were, it seems clear that the apostle put the question supposing them to be disciples of Christ—believers who had been baptized into His name, who had therefore been born of the Holy Spirit. We see that they were in truth only the followers of John the Baptist— disciples who had not personally entered into the Christian dispensation. But the point, after all, is not what was their spiritual condition, but what was the apostle's intention, what was the purport of his question.

Does not his question indicate the fact that it is possible to be a believer, to be born of the Spirit, and yet not to have the Holy Spirit in the same sense as the apostles received Him on the day of Pentecost?

So we find the same apostle writing to the Galatians, "*Received* ye the Spirit by the works of the law, or by the hearing of faith?" (Galatians 3:2). Faith consists not in working but in receiving.

Compare with this our Lord's words: "Even the Spirit of truth; whom *the world cannot receive*, because it seeth Him not, neither knoweth Him: but ye know Him" (John 14:17), etc. "With the world, want of vision prevented possession. With the disciples the personal presence of the Paraclete brought knowledge, and with that knowledge the power of *more complete reception*" (Canon Westcott).

If many are hindered for want of desire, how many are hindered for want of reception! Here seems to be the difficulty with really earnest souls. There is much asking but little or no blessing, because there is not a corresponding reception. And yet it is through this door—a present believing reception—that the fullness of the Spirit, as well as every other blessing, is to be realized.

Our Lord's direction in this matter is clear and explicit: "Therefore I say unto you, What things soever ye desire, when ye pray, believe that ye receive them, and ye shall have them" (Mark 11:24). That is, "We are to believe, not that we shall one day have what we pray for in a future more or less distant, but that we actually receive it as we pray" (*New Testament Commentary.* Edited by Bishop Ellicott).

To believe that we are receiving is more than to believe that we are desiring and asking. It is when our faith passes from the stage of seeking to that of receiving that the fullness comes.

To ask truly is to ask in Christ's name. When we thus pray we not only ask but also receive. "Hitherto have ye asked nothing in My name: ask, and ye shall receive, that your joy may be full" (John 16:24).

Let us notice our Lord does not say here, "Ask, and it shall be given you." That is true, but He is here speaking of the other side—man's side, of receiving: "Ask, and *ye shall receive.*" True asking will surely be followed or accompanied by an actual and present reception.

But many are perplexed because they fail to recognize the nature of this filling.

Instead of seeking to have more of the Holy Spirit, we should yield ourselves to Him that He might have more of us.

A simple illustration may help us here.

You receive someone into your house, and you let him have possession of one room. It is, let us suppose, the best room in your house, but still you give him only that one room. After a while you let him have another apartment. And so you go on, letting him take room after room, until at last the whole house is in his possession and under his control.

Now in this case what has taken place? It is not that more and more of the man has come into your house, but that more and more of your house has come into his possession.

So let us never forget when we speak of being filled with the Spirit that the blessing consists not in receiving a mere influence or emanation from God. He is a Person. We have received Him. He entered our hearts when we passed from death unto life. We received the personal Holy Spirit when we believed and became converted to Christ. But the blessing consists in this, that we have been brought more completely under His power and control. It is He who has taken a fuller possession of us.

This is to be sanctified wholly. When not only the spirit—the central part of our being, where the work of regeneration *commences*—but when the "whole spirit and soul and body"—every room in the house, so to speak—is yielded up to Him, then it is that we are "full of the Holy Ghost."

But one word by way of caution. In seeking this blessing let us see to it that we do not lose our rest. If we have been brought into the rest of faith, if we have entered into His rest, let us not be allured out of it on any consideration. Nothing is more essential than restfulness if we would wait upon God. But many have so prayed for the "baptism of the Spirit" that they have completely wrestled themselves out of rest. Let us see then that our earnestness does not degenerate into impatient anxiety.

Another warning is needful. Let nothing tempt you to look away from Christ, or lead you to imagine that the blessing you seek is something outside of Him or apart from Him. Remember that "*all* fullness"—therefore the fullness of the Spirit—dwells in Him.

Again, see that you do not set your heart upon getting an experience—some extraordinary *afflatus*. Be willing to rest in God's will. Let Him "take you, break you, and make you"; then He will possess you.

One word as to evidences. Does any one ask, "How shall I know that I have the fullness of the Spirit?" You will be assured of this by knowing it. Compare the two statements in John 14:11 and 20: "*Believe* Me that I am in the Father, and the Father in Me"; "At that day [the day of the Spirit's fullness to you] ye shall *know* that I am in My Father, and ye in Me, and I in you." "You shall come to know, by the teaching of the Spirit, what is for the time a matter of faith only." At that day you shall "in that knowledge realize the fullness of your fellowship with Me." The fullness of the Spirit makes Christ to our consciousness a real, indwelling, and all-sufficient Savior. The Spirit never draws away our attention from Christ to any other object. He glorifies Christ. The more we know of the fullness of the Spirit, the more we shall glory in Christ, and the more shall we be occupied with Him. "The dispensation of the Spirit is the revelation of Christ" (Canon Westcott).

APPENDIX

NOTE A, *p.* 51

SUBSTITUTION of Christ. Canon Liddon has a valuable remark in one of his sermons: "'He loved me, and gave Himself for me.' The Eternal Being gave Himself for the creature which His hands had made. He gave Himself to poverty, to toil, to humiliation, to agony, to the cross. He gave Himself *huper emou*, for my benefit; but also *huper emou*, in my place. In this sense of the preposition St. Paul claimed the services of Onesimus as a substitute for those which were due to him from Philemon—*hina huper sou moi diakone* (Cf. Bp. Ellicott on Galatians 3:13). Such a substitution of Christ for the guilty sinner is the ground of the Satisfaction which Christ has made upon the cross for human sin."—*Liddon: "University Sermons,"* p. 239.

NOTE B, *pp.* 47 and 68

"According to Meyer, *sarkinos* designates the unspiritual state of nature which the Corinthians still had in their early Christian minority, inasmuch as the Holy Spirit had as yet changed their character so slightly that they appeared as if consisting of men of flesh still.

"But *sarkikos* expresses a later ascendency of the hostile material nature over the divine principle of which they had been made partakers by progressive instruction. And it is the latter which, as he [Meyer] thinks, the apostle makes the ground of his rebuke. In so far, however, as both epithets are of kindred signification, he could, notwithstanding the distinction between them, affirm 'for ye are yet carnal.'"—*Lange on 1 Corinthians 3*.

"But that the term *sarkinois* is to be here understood relatively, and as not denoting an entire lack of the *pneuma*, is clearly indicated by the phrase, 'As unto babes in Christ.' . . .

"They were *sarkikoi* at first, but not developing their spirituality they became *sarkoiki*"—*Lange*.

According to Delitzsch, "*sarkinos* is one who has in himself the bodily nature and the sinful tendency inherited with it; but *sarkikos* is one whose personal fundamental tendency is this impulse of the flesh."

Bengel quotes Ephraem Syrus: "The apostle calls men who live according to nature *natural*, *psuxikous*; those who live contrary to nature *carnal*, *sarkikous*; but those are *spiritual*, *pneumatikoi*, who even change their nature after the spirit."

NOTE C, *p*. 60

"That the apostle ascribed to man a *pneuma* belonging to his nature is clear from 1 Corinthians 2:11, where he speaks expressly of *pneuma tou anthropou*. It is the principle of knowledge and self-consciousness, the same which he elsewhere terms *nous*; but here designates as *pneuma* in order to draw a parallel between the *Pneuma tou Theou* and the *pneuma tou anthropou*."— *Prof. Dickson on "St. Paul's Use of the Terms Flesh and Spirit*," pp. 22–23.

"The question, whether the natural man has a *pneuma* . . . is to be answered roundly in the affirmative, on the ground of various passages quite unambiguous (such as 1 Corinthians 2:11, 5:4, 6:20, 7:34, Romans 8:16).These passages also give us significant hints as to its nature. It is specifically distinguished from the divine *pneuma*, as it needs comfort and rest (2 Corinthians 2:13, 7:13); it may be defiled and require purification (2 Corinthians 7:1); it is assumed that it needs to be sanctified and preserved (1 Thessalonians 5:23); and the possibility of its not being saved is plainly implied (in 1 Corinthians 5:5)."—*Prof. Dickson (above quoted)*, pp. 56–57.

NOTE D, *p*. 96

"The GREEK AORIST expresses an action or event rounded off and complete in itself. 'A point in the expanse of time,' whether in the past, the present, or the future, but especially in the past." "The aorist tense therefore expresses complete action. It may cover a single act, or a series of acts. If the former, it denotes the act *not as in progress but as complete*. If the latter, it represents the series as concluded, rounded off, wound up, condensed to a point. The aorist always denotes a point in contradistinction to a line. This force is essential to it in all the moods."

NOTE E, *p.* 100

"Christ not only grew in wisdom and stature like other men, but underwent the ordinary process of discipline by which virtue is matured and attains its due reward; He grew ethically, as well as physically and intellectually. He rendered meritorous obedience, and *earned* the crown by enduring the cross (Hebrews 12:2). The *teleiosis* of which the Epistle to the Hebrews speaks (5:9) implies a previous state of relative imperfection: what can this be in One whom we believe to have been sinless?

"It must be considered as negative, not positive; as analogous to the imperfection of the first Adam before he underwent his trial. Virtue, to prove itself such, must be tried; and the severer the trial the greater the result if resistance to sin is successful. The second Adam, like the first, must pass through the furnace. He must be tempted, and overcome the temptation, endure sufferings which culminate in death, 'learn obedience by the things which He suffered' (Hebrews 5:8), and to become 'perfect' (Hebrews 2:10) in a different sense from that in which He was before. He attained the perfection of a proved and triumphant virtue as distinguished from a state of untried innocence. And thus He became fitted, from His own personal experience, to be a 'merciful and faithful High Priest in things pertaining to God.'"—*"Introduction to Dogmatic Theology," by Rev. E. A. Litton, late Fellow of Oriel College, Oxford,* p. 227.